UNLOCKING PURPOSE

Understanding the Will of God for Your Life and Discovering the Greatness of Your Purpose

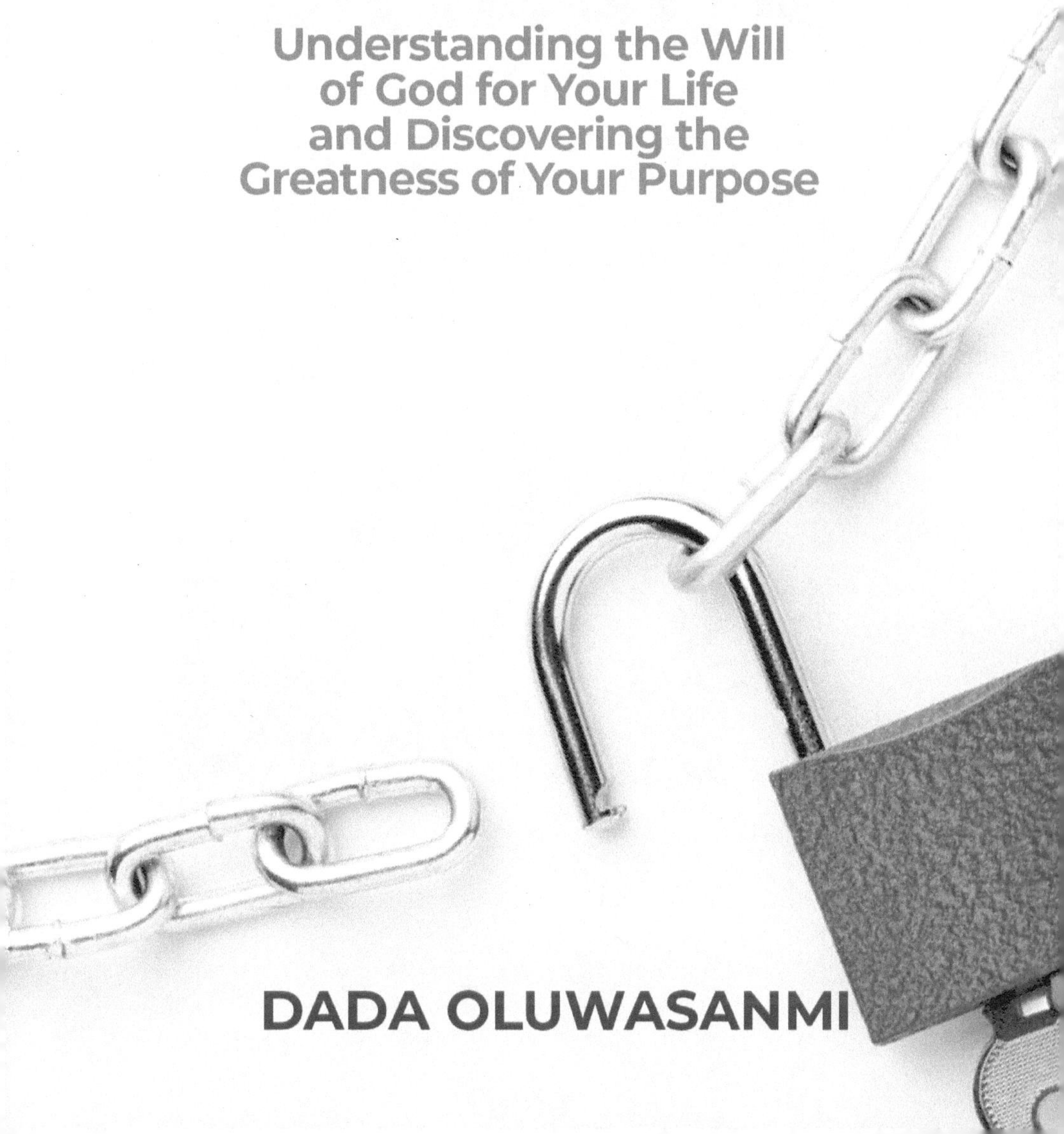

DADA OLUWASANMI

UNLOCKING PURPOSE

Understanding the Will of God for Your Life and Discovering the Greatness of Your Purpose

DADA OLUWASANMI

Unlocking Purpose

ISBN: 978-978-788-230-6

Published in Nigeria by:
Pen-Impact Writing and Publishing Enterprise
16, Adedoyin Rhodes-Vivour Close, Asokoro
FCT, Abuja, Nigeria
Website: www.pen-impact.com
Email: info@pen-impact.com
Tel: +234 701 990 4999

TABLE OF CONTENT

DEDICATION

TO GOD ALMIGHTY, the Monarch of the universe, the Father from whom all blessings flow. To my late sister, Motunrayo Deborah Dada, whose life inspired me and revealed God's faithfulness, even in the darkest moments of my life. To everyone whose desire is to fulfill God's purpose for their lives. I am grateful to all my teachers and mentors whose teachings and mentorship have shaped my life.

INTRODUCTION

OUR SUCCESS IN battles and life depends on our willingness to follow instructions from those with more excellent knowledge and understanding. In a battle scenario, soldiers who ignore their commandant's instructions put themselves at a disadvantage, as the commandant has access to information that they do not. We are the soldiers, and the commandant is God's spirit in us.

The Bible teaches us that there is a spirit within us, and by following that spirit, we can gain a greater understanding of ourselves and our experiences. Therefore, like soldiers in battle, it is in our best interest to heed the instructions of our commandant with instant obedience.

Job 32:8

'There is a spirit in man, and the breath of the Almighty gives him understanding.'

We can deduce from the above scripture that:

Man as an entity is first a spirit. He has a soul and lives in a body. The soul is the seat of intelligence, emotions, and will, while the body is a compartment that houses the soul, and the spirit is the soul's voice. Man should live from the inside to the outside, and whatever inspires man controls him. Understanding is a function of God's breath(spirit) in man, and he draws his inspiration from

God's breath. The spirit looks so intangible but powerful. It is a voice within the soul and is responsible for giving the soul understanding (the proper application of intelligence, emotions, and will).

Living Soul Versus Dead Soul:

Today's world is a mixed multitude of living and dead souls, and these two are contending for the body. The soul is said to be living because of God's breath (Spirit); hence, the body cannot give the soul life (God's intelligence, man's emotion, and will). Adam, the first man created, had a living soul with God's intelligence and will reside in it.

Genesis 2:7

> *"And the LORD God formed man of the dust of the ground and breathed into his nostrils the breath of life, and man became a living soul."*

God also put him in Eden (God's presence) for fellowship, thereby nurturing his soul with God's intents and purposes so his soul can live forever. Adam had the privilege of having a soul saturated with God's intelligence and will, but he lost that privilege to the devil when he disobeyed God's commandment. That disobedience cost him his dominion, and God chased him out of Eden. He lost God's presence, and his soul lost God's intelligence and will. His soul began to feed from the fruit of knowledge of good and evil. This fruit eventually became a seed that produces fruits of knowledge of good and evil from one generation to another. Man's soul now becomes the seat of man's intelligence, will, and emotions. The soul that was meant to produce life now produces death.

Genesis 3:3

"But of the fruit of the tree amid the garden, God has said, "You shall not eat it, nor shall you touch it, lest you die."

Therefore, the departure of God's Spirit from a soul makes the soul a dead soul. Man's rebellion to God's instruction makes his soul dead. Today, everyone born of a woman has an empty soul, and the environment they grew up in imposes will and intelligence on them. The soul now needs redemption to live again, and that redemption is in and through Christ. It is imperative to understand the content of the spirit, just as we know what the soul contains. The spirit is the voice of the soul, and it communicates the will or intentions of His principal to the soul. So, if God's Spirit lives in us, His will becomes our inspiration.

Through the help of the Holy Spirit, I have written a book to guide you toward understanding God's purpose for your life. Through its pages, you will gain insight into your obligations to God and how to respond to His will for your life. With clear and concise language, this book will help you discover the meaning behind God's plan for you and how to live a fulfilling life through His teachings.

As you read this book, keep an open mind and heart, and reflect on how to apply these lessons to your daily life. Remember, discovering your purpose and fulfilling your obligations to God is an ongoing journey, and this book is simply a tool to help you along the way.

Chapter One

THE PURSUIT OF GOD

According to biblical scripture, man is a unique and divinely created being fashioned in the likeness of God. With the declaration, "*Let us create man in our image, according to our likeness." (Genesis 1:26a)*, we know man's creation was a collective decision of God the Father, Son, and the Holy Spirit. The prophetic psalmist, David, captures this sense of awe and wonder about the nature and identity of man.

Psalm 8:4

> *"What is man that You are mindful of him, And the son of man that You visit him? For You have*

made him a little lower than the angels, And You have crowned him with glory and honour. You have made him to have dominion over the works of Your hands; You have put all things under his feet."

According to David's understanding, man's true identity comprises several facets. Firstly, man has a source - namely God - and therefore exists as a spiritual being with a physical body. Additionally, God has granted man dominion over all He has created and imbued him with a sense of purpose. Man is not an afterthought creation; his substance already exists in God's mind. In other words, God had an ideal man in His mind with the mandate to execute His will.

Unfortunately, man lost control, authority, and dominion when rebelling against God's commandments. Rebellion destroyed the knowledge of God in his heart and caused him to lose his way. Man became unable to navigate his domain through the will of God and lost his authority of dominion.

Despite this, God had a redemption plan fueled by His faithful nature and omniscience. Knowing that the devil would introduce rebellion to man, God had implemented a plan allowing man to regain his authority, access God's will, retain God's knowledge in his heart, and be empowered to do God's will. All these possibilities would be man's reality, but he must make up his mind to seek his creator and accept redemption through Christ, the only way to approach God.

A Call to Redemption

THE REDEEMER BECKONS to all who want to regain rest because there is rest for a soul disconnected from His source. You know, sometimes, when I attend funerals, and I hear the preacher or people say to the dead, 'May the soul of our beloved brother, sister, father, mother, or friend rest in peace.' I find it challenging to say Amen, especially when the departed soul did not find rest and peace with God when they were alive. Jesus said,

Matthew 11:28

> *"Come to Me, all who are weary and heavily burdened [by religious rituals that provide no peace], and I will give you rest [refreshing your souls with salvation]."*

Jesus tells us that there is no eternal rest in heaven if we do not receive rest from Him while on earth. So, He bids us come to receive the rest that will make us be at peace with God. How did Christ give us rest? Christ leads us back to the Father, but before He presents us to the Father, He first removes our burden of sin and the weight of guilt in our hearts and exchanges it with His burden (the Father's will).

The Father's will restore rest to our souls

We can refocus our lives and seek redemption through Christ and His ultimate sacrifice. By accepting Christ's redemption, we can enter into a relationship with God and fulfill our ultimate purpose. In essence, redemption becomes the foundation for our search for God.

A Call to Seek the Father's Kingdom

AFTER HE RESTORES rest and peace, He made another call, which is the purpose of His redemption. God's original intent was not to take us to heaven but to make the kingdom of this world the kingdom of our God and His Christ. The ideal man in the mind of God was to bring the reign of the King and His culture to the earth He created. It is this very Kingdom (personality) man lost to rebellion in Eden that Jesus calls us to seek.

Matthew 6:33

> *But first and most importantly, seek (aim at, strive after) His kingdom and His righteousness [His way of doing and being right—the attitude and character of God], and all these things will be given to you also.*

Jesus is reminding us again that the Father's will we receive is what we should continuously seek. In other words, the Father's will is His attitude, character, perspectives, intentions, and purposes. Every day, we must seek His kingdom and righteousness in every matter.

The Knowledge of God

NOW THAT WE have access to the Father, we can seek Him. To honestly know God, fostering a relationship with Him through fellowship and an unyielding hunger for His presence is crucial. This hunger ignites our pursuit of a more profound comprehension of His will as we seek Him with childlike curiosity and inquisitiveness.

Every child is hungry for knowledge. Children are curious, which is the attitude we must bring to God's presence. The eagerness of a child to seek knowledge is truly remarkable. I witnessed this in my six-year-old daughter, who continuously amazes me with her complex and thought-provoking questions. She tirelessly seeks answers to her inquiries, questioning everyone around her until she receives a satisfactory response.

There is a paradox in our human nature when seeking knowledge about something. Specifically, we often have a strong desire to know more about a particular thing or person, but we tend to neglect the source of that knowledge or person. We see this in many aspects of life, including relationships. For example, a young man may be interested in getting to know a lady but may need to pay more attention to her background or where she comes from. Instead, he may seek information from friends or acquaintances without asking the lady about her life story.

This tendency is also reflected in how we approach our relationship with God. Although we may want His blessings and provision for our lives, we often get too caught up in the distractions of everyday life to seek Him out and truly get to know Him better. We might attend church or read religious texts, but we don't try to connect with God on a deeper level. It's almost as if we are treating God like a distant relative whose name we know but whose story we have never bothered to learn.

The question, then, is how can we break out of this pattern and truly get to know God on a personal level? Like any relationship, it requires intentionality and effort. We must set aside time to fellowship with God in prayer, meditation, and reflection. We need to learn about God's character consciously and in different ways, such as by reading the Bible or other Christian literature, attending worship services, or discussing faith with others. And perhaps most importantly, we must approach our relationship with God with an open heart and a sense of wonder and curiosity, as if we are meeting Him for the first time.

In doing so, we can experience God's love and provision. We can learn to see Him as a source of blessings and our Creator, Father, and Friend. And in doing so, we can start to break down the paradox that has kept us from truly knowing the source of all that is good and true.

My daughter, who is six years old, continues to wow me with the complexity of the questions she poses and the eagerness with which she seeks solutions to those concerns. She asks everyone around her the same question until she gets an answer that satisfies her curiosity and her need for information. My daughter questioned the validity of my theology regarding God's existence, and I always fall back on the Holy Spirit for an answer.

The reality is that the pursuit of knowledge or an understanding of a mystery predisposes us to form feelings of fondness, great desire, or aversion for the result of our search.

My daughter seems to notice our frequent discussions about God, Jesus, and the Holy Spirit within our family and with those around us. I want to believe that her observation has deepened her curiosity about God.

She has approached us countless times asking thought-provoking questions, and each time we answer her questions, we also make her understand that we do not have all the answers to her questions. Even when she gets satisfactory answers to her curiosity, she should not think we have all the answers. You know how children always believe that their parents know everything. So, we redirect her to ask God and believe that God is not a respecter of persons; He speaks to everyone who cares to hear from Him. We realized that my daughter's intimacy with God has increased, and she now has more questions. If you do not deeply understand God's word, you may find that you cannot answer her questions.

For instance, what do you say when your daughter asks, *"Did Jesus ever speak in tongues?" and if speaking in tongues is our prayer language to communicate with God?"*. I was studying the word, preparing for a message to be delivered in church when she came into the room to ask these questions. My wife, out of anger or maybe as a way to escape the questions, yelled at my daughter, *"Leave your dad alone; he is preparing a sermon."* I looked at my daughter and smiled. In my mind, I said, Holy Spirit, help me, and when I saw that she would not let go until her curiosity was satisfied, the Holy Spirit whispered the answer to my ears, and I told her, and she went away, *"Hmmm, now I understand."* I told this story to bring to our attention that God grants our righteous desires. God has all the answers to what we call mysteries. God has answers to all the why, how, who, and when questions in our hearts.

It is a curious paradox of human nature that we often desire to know something better than its source. This is especially evident in relationships, where a young man may be interested in a lady without considering her background or family. Instead, he may seek information from friends or other sources, neglecting the very source of that lady's being.

Similarly, in modern marriages, the bridegroom may meet his father-in-law for the first time on the day of engagement or introduction. But is this not also true in our relationship with God? We often seek His blessings and providence without genuinely seeking to know Him as our source. We become preoccupied with the distractions of life, allowing them to draw our attention away from the One who sustains us. We must rediscover that desire to know God, seek Him with a pure heart, and bask in His love and grace. Let us not neglect our trustworthy source but instead draw near to God and find peace in His presence.

As believers, it is essential to recognize that having a relationship with God is not solely based on logic, reasoning, science, or metaphysics. Our role as God's creation is to intentionally seek to understand His plans and purposes for our lives. Following after something to capture or gain control of it is known as "pursuit." The pursuit of God should not be about trying to control Him but rather about allowing Him to take control of both the present and the future in order to fulfil His plans for us.

Our aim should not be to manipulate God into doing our will but to align our desires with His. Ultimately, our knowledge of God should lead us to live out His will daily.

Sadly, however, too many of us become sidetracked by our ambitions and lose sight of the importance of seeking God above all else.

The pursuit of God is a deeply personal journey that is driven by a powerful longing within individuals to discover more about God's nature and purpose. This journey is ongoing and never-ending as God reveals Himself to those who seek Him. However, it should be remembered that God is eternal and beyond human comprehension.

Nevertheless, anyone who earnestly wishes to pursue God will be able to experience Him in their life. As we follow God's ways on a daily basis, seeking His guidance and leadership through His Spirit, we will come to understand His purposes for our lives. This understanding will bring fulfilment and purpose to our lives and will enable us to live in accordance with God's will.Ultimately, the service and devotion to God's ways are more than a mere belief in His existence; it is a profound and transformative journey that brings us closer to God and deepens our understanding of His nature and purpose.

God's existence is a reality irrespective of our beliefs. It is not an ideology, meaning you can believe it. However, genuinely knowing God goes beyond mere belief. One can fully comprehend His being through experiencing and gaining knowledge of the realities of God's existence.

This experience creates an insatiable urge within us to learn more and know more about God. Despite God's status as having no beginning or end, He reveals Himself to those who desire to pursue Him. Therefore, every pursuit of God begins with a desire or an affection for Him.

We are not serving God because we believe in His existence; we serve and follow His ways because we know He lives and has plans for our lives. God reveals His purposes for our lives as we follow His ways daily and provides us leadership through His Spirit.

Job 32:8 (AMP)

> *"But there is [a vital force] a spirit [of intelligence] in man, and the breath of the Almighty gives men understanding."*

The word breath means spirit. So, the breath of God is divine intellect and inspiration. It is like a wind that blows us in different directions at a time. I have never seen a man who followed the leading of God or His will and came out stupid at the end. God's will provides us with the spiritual intelligence that surpasses all intelligence.

Through God's guidance, man discovers the reason for his being and the meaning behind his life. Every time I have the opportunity to talk about purpose, I tell people that God's purpose is man's purpose. So, whenever we choose to follow God's leading, we also choose to fulfil

His purpose, which is our purpose. Introducing this book, I made it known to us that the spirit conveys will, intentions and the ideal state of a being, but let me also add that everything the spirit conveys presents itself to us as thought. The thoughts became words. God leads us by His thoughts (reasonings, logos, and words), and we understand His leading by His Rhema (the revealed word). Our purpose, which is God's intention, is located in the revealed word. Therefore, a man's purpose is dependent on what he truly believes.

Proverbs 23:7A

"As a man thinks in his heart, so he is."

The word "heart" refers to your passion(beliefs), appetite, and mind (activity of will). Therefore, if my appetite is God and all He wants for me, that is what I become. Finding God and cultivating a relationship with Him should be a priority for anyone who wants to live a meaningful life. If what a man thinks is what he becomes, he must think like God to become God-like, and this should be our ultimate goal. Our search for God allows us to learn about His word, precepts, ways, and nature.

However, we must ask ourselves an important question: Who can understand God's methodology and principles for living a fulfilling life? David, in one of his psalms, gave us an insight into this question.

Psalm 24: 3-6

> *"Who may ascend the mountain of the LORD? Who may stand in his holy place? The one who has clean hands and a pure heart, who does not trust in an idol or swear by a false god. They will receive blessing from the LORD and vindication from God their Saviour. Such is the generation of those who seek him, who seek your face, God of Jacob".*

We cannot engage God with uncleanness and expect Him to draw nearer to us. Our curiosity to know Him leaves us responsible for eschewing evil and corruption. An unregenerated soul cannot experience the essence of God. The study of God does not result in disclosing God's essential nature, which explains why it is highly conceivable to be a teacher of the Bible with all of the degrees in theology and still not receive a glimpse of His essence, glory, and beauty that produce transformation. The validity of man is in the very nature of God that he exhibits, yet we all lost this reality when the first man (Adam) fell in the Garden of Eden.

Salvation Precedes the Discovery of Purpose

MAN LOST HIS essence, glory, and God's Spirit and image after the fall in the Garden of Eden. He had everything taken away from him. He was naked and lacked dignity. An eternal schism existed between man's Spirit and God's Spirit. As a result of his rebellious actions, man became subject to demonic attacks and other forms of persecution. The Devil was successful in dethroning humankind from his positions as king and priest. Man's rebellion unleashed Hell and its terror, and he lost control of the things designed for his benefit.

Man lost control over sin, making disobedience the default setting for all children born of a woman. According to the Bible, after eating the fruit of the tree of knowledge of good and evil, man was forbidden the right to eat the fruit of the tree of life. Death came into the picture as the reward for man's rebellion. No surprise; the Bible states that no man is good. There is nothing good about a dead human being. Every attempt to restore man through atonement for sin with animal sacrifice failed. God raised among men kings, priests, and prophets to reveal the way to salvation by keeping ordinances and regulations with the provision to atone for every sin committed by providing various types of sacrifice. Even this could not bring back life—God's life—into man.

Finally, as His prophet had predicted, man attained grace in God's eyes.Jesus Christ the Messiah, God's only begotten son became the ransom in exchange for the dead or spiritually dead position or mode that man had been in since the fall of the first man (Adam). Jesus absorbed all of the blame for sin, both past and present (of everyone born after His death), and He carried it to the cross, where He was murdered for our transgression.

He who knew no sin died for humanity so that humanity could be at peace with God.

1 Peter 2:24 (AMP)

> *"He personally bore our sins in His own body on the tree [as on an altar and offered Himself on it], that we might die (cease to exist) to sin and live to righteousness."*

His wounds have healed you. Jesus' bruises and the shedding of His blood were the only atonement for our sins. We are restored, and His death also imparts righteousness on those who believe in the death and resurrection of Jesus Christ, the only begotten of the Father.

Romans 10:10 (AMP)

> *"For with the heart a person believes (adheres to, trusts in, and relies on Christ) and thus is justified (found righteous, acceptable to God), and with the mouth, he confesses (openly and freely expresses his faith) and confirms [his] salvation."*

Salvation entails a belief and confession of what we believe. By this, the breath of God comes into man and repositions him for all that he lost to rebellion. Man regains control (dominion) over sin and obtains deliverance from the burden of darkness.

We must remember that salvation is a gift. Hence, it is up to us to decide how to use the gift—our salvation. The gift of salvation is similar to sowing a seed in the ground (our heart), which needs to receive care from God's word to produce the fruit of righteousness. Our path in pursuing God begins with accepting this gift, and our experiences or encounters as we pursue God depend on how we use the salvation we have received. If redemption bestows Christ's righteousness on me, I must wear righteousness as a garment wherever I go. There are some areas where I won't go because of the clothing of righteousness, and there are doors I won't open because they will lead me to disaster. Consciously living a righteous life by God's grace places me at the centre of God's plan for my life.

Jesus is the Way, the Truth, and the Life

Isaiah. 43:19

> *"Behold, I will do a new thing; it will spring forth now; shall you not know it? I will make a way in the wilderness and rivers in the desert."*

LIFE WITHOUT JESUS is nothing more than a jungle adventure. It's like walking through the desert without a compass to guide us. Life without Christ is like anticipating a pool of water in the desert. When we accept Christ as our Lord and Saviour, He points us towards our source (God, the Father). His life within us connects us to the Father's Spirit (the Holy Spirit). The Holy Spirit is that river that flows within us, renewing our souls amid a thirsty land. God spoke to Isaiah, *"I will do something new". Isaiah 43:19*

What? I thought there was nothing new under the sun. If you have not yet received Jesus, He is the new personality God sends you today. He is the gateway to everything new, peculiar, and unique you will ever experience.

John 14:6

> *"I am the way, the truth, and the life," Jesus said to him. "No one approaches the Father except through me."*

As Jesus informed Thomas, He also reminds you that He is the way out of a meaningless life, perplexity, and depressing thoughts that cloud your mind. The truth is that we have no idea how to live. We are yet to learn what life has in store for us or where it takes us. Jesus is the only compass that will lead us to our destination. Many of us now believe we know what we're doing, only to discover that everything we've gathered is nothing but shadows as we progress through life. This verse shows that Jesus is the only route and compass that can guide us through life's journey. In Hebrew, the word "way" (*hodos*) refers to a course of action, a way of thinking, feeling, and deciding. Our actions, thoughts, feelings, and decisions all impact the results of our lives.

Thus, it is essential to understand that there are mental patterns, a course of life, conduct, and decisions to follow as we go through life. Jesus must be at the centre of this because He is the way. We must imitate Christ to fulfil the purpose He intends for our lives. In John 14:6, Jesus said, *"I am the way, the truth, and the life. No one comes to the Father except through me."* His manner, conduct, and thought must be our manner, conduct, and mind. *"I tell you the truth: You cannot see God's kingdom unless you are born again." John 3:3*

To be reborn implies going back to the beginning (Revelation 2:4-5). The life you've begun with God, yes! God creates life at conception. We were once a seed in our mothers' wombs, and God's breath gives us life. God is the source of that life. We must surrender that life to Him for Him to reveal His plan for the life He has given us. To repent and give up the previous sin-filled life is to be born again. Without true repentance, there is no forgiveness. Jesus did not stop there; He declared that seeking His kingdom is not enough; we must strive to enter God's kingdom.

John 3:5

> *Jesus answered, "I assure you that unless one is born of water and the Spirit, he cannot enter the kingdom of God."*

The baptism by immersion, which symbolises death, is what Jesus was talking about here. He also calls our attention to the fact that if we are dead to the world and all its deeds, we are quickened by His Spirit to live His life. If a man used to commit adultery, receiving the life of Christ makes him dead to adultery, and the Spirit of Jesus now quickens him to live like Christ.

Chapter Two

MAN'S ULTIMATE PURPOSE

God's eternal plan for us is to conform to His image—His nature and character—for this is the primary reason for which the plan of God for man thrives. This conformity to God's image and likeness begins with salvation. It grows as we live daily, following the footprint of our Master Jesus Christ and meditating on His word. God has two compartments: His word (spoken or written) and His glory. These two are inseparable. When we conform to His word, we behold His glory. We must recognise that when God communicates with us, He reveals His will. As a result, every time we obey God's word, we fulfil His purpose for our lives. Obedience to

God's word helps us accomplish His objectives for our lives. While we await specific instructions from the Lord regarding our assignments, we must seek God's will on every matter.

Romans 8:29

> *For whom He did foreknow, He also did predestinate to be conformed to the image of His Son, that He might be the firstborn among many brethren.*

From this scripture, it is clear that God's purpose for man is to conform to His image and likeness. Reflecting His likeness presents us as perfect before God, and this is the perfection to which the scriptures encourage us. The image of God (man) is ideal beauty, and that is what we are. When Jesus encouraged us to be perfect as our heavenly Father (God) is perfect, He meant that we were created with such a perfect beauty of God's glory—His image—and that is what people should see us express or reflect.Being created in the image of God means that we share God's perfection and holiness, which our lives demonstrate to the world. Many of us are uncomfortable with the word "perfect," believing that God expects us to be identical to Him. To be perfect does not mean we should be like God; instead, we should exhibit His nature and character. God is Spirit, and we are not; we are human beings with God's Spirit. The Spirit of God in us empowers us to exhibit God's essence and character, commonly known as the fruit of the Spirit.

Hebrew 12:14

> *Strive to live in peace with everybody and pursue that consecration and holiness without which no one will ever see the Lord. (AMP)*

We see holiness as the only weapon for finding peace with God and people. It is what brings us together and makes us one with God. In other words, we are one with Christ; we have been infused with God to the point where we are inseparable. This is significant because it releases God's power into our lives, allowing us to fulfil our unique purpose or His assignment.

God's Will: Man's Assignment

"Commitment to the will of God—the purpose for which we are designed—offers freedom to become the persons we are meant to be."

Charles E. Hummel

MAN WAS CREATED in God's image, for God's glory, and has a glorious destination. God invested everything in man to bring God's glory to the earth. He glorified those whom He called (exalted, elevated), which suggests that there is a call to duty for all those called.

Roman 8:30

> *"And having chosen them, He called them to come to Him, and He gave them right standing with Himself, and He promised them His glory."*

God has an assignment for everyone, predicated on one purpose: to show His glory. God has endowed us with talent and potential (inherent abilities) and His Spirit (God's abilities). All of these, when completely harnessed, will produce a significant outcome. These significant outcomes are God's glory. There is glory, honour, and power in a purposefully fulfilled life. We must remember that the power, prestige, and glory men may ascribe to us as we obey His call (assignment) are not ours but His. He deserves the glory.

Revelation 4:11

> *"Thou art worthy, O Lord, to receive glory, honour, and power; for thou hast created all things, and for thy pleasure"*

We must recognise that God is not a taskmaster. He will not ask you to give Him what He has not given you. Man has everything he needs to fulfil God's call on his life. When we fulfil our primary purpose, which is to conform to God's image by obeying His commands, we reign over principalities and powers. (Ephesians 1:2–14; Colossians 1:15–18) .God calls everyone and gives them something. Jesus told the parable of the talents; the Master gave different measures of talent to individuals based on their potentials or abilities and the turnover with the talents given, except for one of them, who buried his talent and produced nothing. The Master equips all those He calls, but the choice is ours to profit from it or not. The call of God on our lives envelops what I call the precise will or directions of God for our lives.

Numerous books are written about us (Psalm 40:7 and Hebrews 10:7). Let us examine the following Bible passages to determine the truth regarding God's purpose for an individual, as Christ is the paradigm of every purpose given to any man.

Psalm 40:5

"O Lord, my God, you have done many wonders for us. You have no equal. If I tried to recite all your wonderful deeds, I would never come to the end of them."

God's wonders for us are encrypted in His plans, which also signify His will for us, so those who seek God diligently stand a chance to fulfil God's purpose. The more we chase after God, the more He reveals His plans, will, and instructions.

John 5:19-20

"So, Jesus explained, I tell you the truth, the son can do nothing alone. He does what he sees the Father doing. Whatever the Father does, the Son also does. For the Father loves the Son and shows

him everything He is doing. The Father will show him how to do even greater works than healing this man. Then you will be genuinely astonished". We have access to never-ending wonders due to our obedience to what the Father is doing—performing God's will. No wonder John the Beloved put it in the last chapter and verse of the book of John 21:25, saying, "Jesus also did many other things. If they were all written down, I suppose the world would be too small to hold all the volumes that would be written".

Let's go a little deeper.

Psalm 40:6

"You take no delight in sacrifices or offerings." Now that you made me listen (You have given me a body), I finally understand you don't require burnt offerings or sin sacrifice."

God is prophesying concerning Jesus through David. At the same time, communicating His will to us, who would become the heirs of salvation, He is not interested in sacrifices, burnt offerings, or sin offerings. We must understand that God's word is His will, commands, and blessings. John 1:1, "*In the beginning was the word, and the word was with God and the word was God*", and in verse fourteen, the scriptures say, "The word became flesh (human) and dwells among us (made His home among us)."

He was full of unfailing love and faithfulness, and we have seen His Glory, the Glory of the Father's one and only Son. God is interested in us manifesting His word and living by His word. Going against God's directions for our lives and being ardent in mundane vineyard operations will be equivalent to presenting unacceptable offerings or what the psalmist called sin sacrifices. Sin offerings are services offered to God in disguise to cover up our disobedience to His desire for us. The Lord delights in the sacrifice that encourages our adherence to God's instructions. No amount of religious sacrifice or service can substitute for reasonable or acceptable sacrifices or services.

Romans 12:1-2 (AMP)

> *I appeal to you, therefore, brethren, and beg of you in view of [all] the mercies of God, to make a decisive dedication of your bodies [presenting all your members and faculties] as a living sacrifice, holy (devoted, consecrated) and well pleasing to God, which is your reasonable (rational, intelligent) service and spiritual worship. Do not be conformed to this world (this age), [fashioned after and adapted to its external, superficial customs], but be transformed (changed) by the [entire] renewal of your mind [by its new ideals and its new attitude], so that you may prove [for yourselves] what is the good and acceptable and perfect will of God, even the thing which is good and acceptable and perfect [in His sight for you].*

A holy sacrifice is a sacrifice that is one with God. It is in alignment with God's will. We can see from the above scriptures that God is not after any services or sacrifices. Many activities believers embark on in our churches today are mere activities or sacrifices that do not align with God's will or purpose for their lives, and this is an enormous tragedy. A brother walked up to me in church after the service and poured his mind on his love for Christ and wanting to join the church workforce. I told him, "Brother, it is good to love God and have passion for the things of God, but it is expedient for you to ask God how He wants you to work for Him."

The church is struggling today because we have a lot of round pegs in square holes. We have zealous brethren who lack understanding of their assignment in God's house. Some pastors even make it worse by asking people to join any department they like, as if God's assignment or will is a function of likeness. God's will often does not appeal to our senses, but the truth is that we can do His will. Many think that it is easy to work for God. Working for God necessitates asking the Lord. It begins with intimacy with the Father.

He knows our frames and what we are capable of. One thing that is not negotiable with God is effective and efficient service; these go hand in hand with our capacity, which God knows. We cannot be in total discord with God's will and claim or maintain the idea that we are working for Him. Jesus stated in Matthew 7:22 that, *"...on the last day, many would cry to Him, "In your name, we raised the dead, healed the sick, and did many miracles." Jesus responded to them, "Depart from me, you workers of iniquity."*

Rebellion against God's will is wickedness. Paul, the Apostle, admonishes us in Romans 12:2 not to imitate the habits or practices of this world. He advised us not to take our cues for how to live from this world but rather from the word of God. God's word is God's character, behaviour, and way of living (custom). Doing God's will was what brought about transformation. Knowing God's will but failing to act on it is similar to having knowledge that cannot transform us. God's purpose is not just to be known but to be done. Many are already informed about their purpose, but that information has not been able to transform their lives because they fail to fulfil that purpose. The difference between information and transformation is "doing". Every time we act on information by doing or applying it to what it addresses, we'll experience transformation.

Psalm 40:7

> *"Then I said, "Look, I have come as is written about me in the scriptures: I take joy in doing your will, my God, for your instructions are written on my heart."*

Our entire life's journey is a script written in God's handwriting. It cannot be altered by any force in the heavens, on the earth, or underneath it. The tragedy is that not many people are working following God's instructions in their hearts. Their entire life is already figured out, either by themselves or by a third party who does not have a glimpse of God's instructions in their heart (Spirit). It is imperative to note that God's will for man is the revealing word of wisdom from God into our soul.

According to the revelation of God's word in the book of Revelation 20:12,

"I also saw the dead, great and small; they stood before the throne, and books were opened. Then, another book was opened, which is the Book of Life. And the dead were judged (sentenced) by what they had done [their whole way of feeling and acting, their aims and endeavours] by what was recorded in the books". (AMP)

These scriptures confirm that there are volumes of books already written, and God will judge our conduct, motives, and endeavours according to His records written in those books. God's Spirit reveals and instructs us based on His intentions.God reveals the details of our assignment, revealing them precept upon precept, line upon line, as we delight ourselves in the Lord. Are we willing to delight ourselves in doing and following

God's will and intentions for our lives, or do we want to continue in an outright display of rebellion against God's will?

God's will for us is just like His promises in the scriptures. All of those promises have conditions attached, so obeying the conditions is also God's will, and that obedience releases the blessing He promised. Without God putting our names on those promises, we put our names by faith and confess the promises to be ours, so they become ours. For instance, it is the will of God for us to live in abundance of everything good; it is also one of His promises in the scriptures. Therefore, God's written or spoken word is His will.

The other perspective to knowing God's will for our lives is that it is not about us having good intentions or motives but receiving a leading from God by the Holy Spirit on our good intentions. David desired to build a tabernacle for God, but it was not righteous. A righteous desire aligns with God's intentions. God told Him your son would build me a house.

1 Chronicles 17:11–14, and 2 Samuel 7:13–14: "For when you die and join your ancestors, I will raise one of your sons and make his kingdom strong." He is the one who will build a house—a temple—for me, and I will secure his throne forever. I will be his Father, and he will be my son. I will never take my favour away from him, as I took it from the one who ruled before you."Solomon

fulfilled that prophesy because he is one of David's sons. God knows in His mind that Solomon will build him the house, yet He told David, "I will raise one of your sons."

There are two brothers in a church. They both love the Lord, are fervent in the Spirit, and operate in the gifts of the Holy Spirit. They were both serving in the church until one day; the Lord spoke to one of them to start a ministry and separate himself from the ministry he is currently serving. He narrated his encounter with God to his friend, spoke to his pastor, and was released to start a church. A few months later, his friend had a misunderstanding with the pastor and then decided in his heart to leave and start his ministry. Of course, it is evident from this story who does God's will among the two brothers. God's will is not a function of our gifts or qualifications. God's will only work out His eternal purposes for individuals as He preordained. He qualifies those He called.

This misery explains most of the disappointments and failures we often encounter in life, unknown to many of us. We ask ourselves, "What does my neighbour or friend know that I do not know that gives him or her an advantage I do not have?"It wasn't an accident or a stroke of luck, and that is, if there is anything like luck at all, I would like to bring it to our notice that the best way to be on the side of luck is to be in the will of God constantly.

Romans 8:28

We are assured and know that [God being a partner in their labour] all things work together and are [fitting into a plan] for good to and for those who love God and are called according to [His] design and purpose.

God's will is not logical. It is not deductive reasoning; sometimes, it defiles the intellectual approach, but it will never contradict God's word. So, the heart requires illumination to grasp the will of God as we journey in our walk with the Lord. Whenever I think about how accepting the will of God has profited my life, it always reminds me of the Pauline prayers to the Ephesians:

Ephesians 1:16-20

I have never stopped thanking God for you. I pray for you constantly, asking God, the glorious Father of our Lord Jesus Christ, to give you spiritual wisdom and understanding so that you might grow in your knowledge of God. I pray that your hearts will be flooded with light so you can understand the wonderful future he has promised to those he called. I want you to realise what a rich and glorious inheritance he has given to his people. I pray that you will begin to understand the incredible greatness of his power for those of us who believe in him. The same mighty power raised Christ from the dead and seated him in the place of honour at God's right hand in the heavenly realms.

I remember these scriptures because I realised that what prevents many people from accepting or doing the will of God is ignorance or lack of understanding. If a child knows that putting his hands in fire will hurt him, I don't think he will ever do so. I also discovered that many have missed their miracle because of this. By the way, our obedience to God's instructions (will) produces the miracles we earnestly desire.It is essential to note that every one of God's instructions (will) as we journey with Him is to work out His ultimate purpose for our lives. We must know that the Devil is our enemy with the ultimate objective of derailing us from doing the will of God. He has no written plan for your life, but his role is to steal, take away, and destroy what God has written concerning you.

The Devil's agenda is to manipulate and shorten the glorious destiny God has planned for humanity; he does this by introducing sin (rebellion) into the world. There is no vacuum in life. Either we are fulfilling God's ordination for our lives, or we remain co-labourers with the Devil in destroying what God has created and ordained for His glory, which includes you. It's all a function of who is in the driver's seat of your life. Is Christ at the centre of your life or the enemy (the Devil)? I encourage you to accept Christ into your life. Submit your will to Him, and you will never regret what you did.

Chapter Three

DISCOVERING YOUR PURPOSE

God's purpose for each person is unique, as evidenced by the various species and elements He created. Trees, plants, animals, the sun, moon, and stars each play a unique role in the ecosystem. Man, as the express image of God, is not exempt from having unique purposes. The entire human race is analogous to a body with various parts designed for different functions; you and I are the parts that make up the whole body, each with our own unique assignment or functionality.Our lives count in the measure of times and seasons, and it displays God's wisdom in setting creation in order. Imagine what would have happened if we all had equal ability to do things irrespective of time, location, and season. Will that not create a crisis, and then who leads who? Therefore, our assignment puts us in a class of our own, and that is leadership. When we have fully internalised this reality, we will understand that our lives transcend the demands of our survival instinct, which frequently causes a misplacement of priority in the scheme of the things we believe are essential to our fulfilment in life.

Many of us view life as primarily consisting of achieving specific goals, such as having a successful profession, getting married, starting a family, being wealthy, and obtaining material possessions. Our definition of success reflects this paradigm when discussing living a successful life. These things bring up our feelings, but they cannot fill the void in our souls. The only thing that can truly satisfy our souls is to find our mission in life and work towards realising it.

Ask yourself these questions: What exactly is the purpose of my existence? Who am I, and why was I created in the first place? The degree to which you answer these questions daily reveals whether you live a fulfilled life. Humans are made outside time and transported into it to accomplish a time-bound assignment. In other words, we do not have eternity to accomplish God's purpose for our lives; therefore, it becomes crucial to discover what purpose is and then propagate it.

Our assignment is the glory, honour, and praise we owe to our creator while alive on earth. Only the living can praise God; the dead can't give Him praise. There are a significant number of teachings available today on the topic of figuring out one's life's purpose. While many of these teachings have a ring of authenticity, some throw us off balance in bringing clarity to our specific purpose, which is the dilemma we often face when knowing or discovering our purpose.

Many are looking for a formula that solves the confusion around purpose. Some are consulting pastors, mentors, coaches, and consultants to help them figure out their purpose in life. A couple of schools of thought interpret purpose differently depending on an individual's beliefs about what man's specific purpose should be. Some believe that our talents and gifts determine our calling. Some individuals misinterpret their acquired skills (career) and potential as their purpose.

Even though we need our potential to fulfil our purpose, it does not represent our purpose. Our purpose gives meaning to our potential, gifts, skills, and careers, and it serves as the compass that directs how we use our talents. Finding one's purpose begins with having an intimate relationship with God. He communicates His will as an instruction that must be adhered to in order to generate an outcome that God has already predestined. That outcome is our purpose.

Our assignment is to do God's will in all that we aspire to do. It is an instruction from the Master that takes a man through the seasons of his life. It is man's compass, given to him by God, to navigate through destiny. There is a predestination for man, and God's assignment for him takes him to that predestination. This necessitates closeness with God.

Ephesians 1:11

> *"In Him, we also were made [God's] heritage [portion], and we obtained an inheritance; for we had been foreordained [chosen and appointed beforehand] by His purpose, who works out everything in agreement with the counsel and design of His [own] will."*

Our lives are much like a play that has been written but is just waiting to be performed. God knows every relationship that will play a part in producing that screenplay. Everything in our lives, including our salvation, is predestined.

We were first and foremost consecrated to God for specific reasons, and this is what sets us apart as His representatives in this generation. The entirety of the human race can be compared to a single body, with several organs serving specialised purposes. You and I are among those organs created for specific functions that separate us.

Speculating, gambling, and moving from one prayer house to the next will not lead us to God's will. God's will is revealed in our intimate walk with Him. Let your desire be, Lord; I want to know you. The knowledge of God gives you a revelation of who you are and what you were made to become. The world has a way of redefining us if we fail to discover the blueprint of our lives that truly defines us.

From birth, our lives are often redefined by the decisions made on our behalf by others, particularly parents or guides. There are things we were not privileged to choose for ourselves, such as parenting, the kind of upbringing, and the environment that nurtured our upbringing. We do not have the privilege to select things such as parenting, the kind of upbringing, or the environment that nurtured our upbringing.There is a possibility that all of our life's critical decisions and choices were made by someone who was not inclined to know what God's mind was in all of the options life threw at us unless we had the privilege of praying for guidance or parents who see themselves as caregivers who must always seek the manual of the product they are caring for from the manufacturer—our source.

In the annals of history, we have inspiring stories of successful people, but not all are fulfilled. The difference is that those who lived a fulfilled life were those whose achievements and exploits aligned with God's ultimate plan for their lives. The lesson here is that our choices—career, spouse, business partner, and so on—can make us either fail or succeed, but God's will (choice) guarantees both success and fulfilment. A successful life is our own and other people's positive remarks about the outcome of our lives, but a fulfilled life is God's remark about the life we live on earth.

Psalm 42:1 (NKJV)

> *"As the deer pants for the water brooks, so pants my soul for You, O God."*

This Psalm captures the desire of a soul that desires to know God. Many believed all was said and done at salvation; salvation provides grace. They didn't see that the soul was still empty and vulnerable, even at salvation. Only our Spirit got recreated and filled with God's Spirit. Therefore, the onus is on us to determine what we want to fill our souls with. So, the psalmist understood this truth and said, "My soul be filled with God." Who is God? God is love; God is His word. A quality relationship with God allows us to hear His voice when He speaks. I do not need to be taught to recognise my wife's voice, even amid noise, because I know her voice. Relationships with God open up conversations that will reveal our assignment to us. Ask God questions about yourself. It is called a prayer of inquiry. Lord, who am I?

Jeremiah 1:5 (AMP)

> *"Before I formed you in the womb, I knew and approved of you [as My chosen instrument], and before you were born, I separated and set you apart, consecrated you, and appointed you as a prophet to the nations."*

God told Jeremiah, "You are a prophet." John the Baptist says, "I am a voice crying in the wilderness, preparing the way for the Lord." Our Lord Jesus said, "I am the good shepherd." The question is, "Who are you"?Before we were formed in our mother's womb, God knew us. Man is the extension of God's glory on earth and is responsible for beautifying the earth with God's glory deposited in him. This glory is expressed in various ways through God's creative power in us (Christ), who embodies God's wisdom and power. Therefore, every human has a flavour of God's glory that we carry because of our ordination in Christ even before the world began. Ultimately, we should all deploy our glory flavours to beautify the earth.

At the beginning of creation, the earth was without form and void, and darkness was on the face of the deep. In Genesis 1:3, God said, "*Let there be light, and there was light.*" And that was the beginning of all things being created. I told you this creation story to help you better understand God's pattern for creating things. The story of creation told in Genesis is being played out once again in the world we live in today when the planet (and the globe) is experiencing extreme levels of darkness, chaos, and confusion. If we believe that God will create another light to dispel the darkness, then this demonstrates that we do not comprehend how God operates.

We are that light tasked with eradicating darkness over human endeavour. Our goal is to bring the glory of God to every corner of the world and fill the world with the glory of God. The light that bursts forth at the moment of creation never returns to where it initially sprang from. Everything that gets its light from that light—the sun, the moon, and the stars—continues to have light after receiving it.

What does it mean for man to comprehend the magnificence of what God has created? It implies that light can sustain everything that comes from it. And in case you were curious about what exactly this light is, I have come to announce that the light you see before you is the incomprehensible wisdom of God, which can only be accessed through Christ, who is in us. It is now clear to us that our mission is to make known the light that resides within us, and we must do so.

The world needs to recognise the multifaceted wisdom that God has placed within each one of us. The unbroken flow of light is what finally extinguishes the night's gloom. We are responsible for turning the switch for that light to provide illumination. The world we live in is losing its shape, expanding into a vacuum, and getting darker by the day. Complete darkness has descended upon all facets of human activity, and all creation, including humans, is quickly adapting to the new norm.

The concepts of righteousness, peace, and love, which were once highly valued as virtues, are changing in the eyes of the world. As a result, each of us is responsible for turning on our switches and consistently applying God's ideas of righteousness, peace, love, and good virtue, as well as His talents (His multifaceted intelligence), to put an end to the crises and anarchy that exist in our world.

Today, the world is gradually becoming formless, void, and dark. Gross darkness has enveloped all aspects of human endeavour and creation, including humans, who conform to darkness at the speed of light. The light that breaks forth at creation never returns to wherever it broke out from. Everything that receives its light from that light (the sun, moon, and stars) still retains it. What does this mean to man—the excellence of God's creation? It means that our light can sustain everything that emanates from it. And in case you are wondering what this light is, I have come to announce to you that this light is the unsearchable wisdom of God that is only accessible through Christ in us. We can now see that our purpose is to shine the light within us. The world needs to see the manifold wisdom of God in us across all sectors. It is the continuity of light that chases out darkness. If we are light, we must turn the switch on for that light to be on.

Our Purpose

Psalms 115:16 (MSB)

> *"The heaven of heavens is for God, but He put us in charge of the earth."*

GOD HAS CALLED us into partnership with Him, entrusting us with the care of the earth He created. John 16:15 says, "*Everything that belongs to my Father is mine, and the universe with all its fullness, the world, and the people who live in it belong to the Lord.*"

We are obligated to assume ownership, be in complete control of the affairs of this world, and grow and spread it with the culture and nature of God's dominion (heaven). Therefore, we aim to align ourselves with God and entirely submit ourselves to Him so that He may create His kingdom on earth through us. The rule of righteousness, peace, and joy in the communion of the Holy Spirit is God's kingdom. We must establish and execute the laws and regulations governing the heavenly government here.Our Lord Jesus Christ provided us with a model for drafting a vision or mission statement that articulates the roles or responsibilities that are specifically ours in His body. Using this template, we can more closely align ourselves with God's singular perspective on our tasks. Using this pattern, we can conclude that Jesus' assignment is also our assignment, and our objectives are identical to Jesus'. Unfortunately, we confused a few ideas, like potential, gift, and career, with our purpose. Before we look at the template our Lord Jesus gives us to use as a model for our purpose, I would like to share some insight regarding potential, gifts, and careers.

Purpose and Potential

POTENTIALS ARE GOD-GIVEN abilities that we all possess. God's ability in humans has been given to us for us to carry out a duty or an assignment. Even eternity will not be enough time to fully realise our potential. It expands with each discovery. When I was growing up, I noticed that I possessed a variety of potential. I use to draw and paint in various styles, play the drums, compose a few poems, and make a few different types of crafts. Now that I've grown, I'm still discovering new things. One day, I sat back and asked myself, "Who am I with all these abilities?" And I learned something about myself that I'm not sure is a strength or a weakness: I don't know how to say 'no' to any assigned duty. I want to give every task my all, and something that looks like me always appears in the process. I made the mistake of misunderstanding my potential for my purpose.

Our potential is God's ability in us that manifests itself every time we face a challenge. Our purpose defines who we are, not who we are not. It is who we are and will be for the rest of our lives. Purpose is the predestined or predetermined end or outcome of a thing. Our purpose does not change. It is who we are today, tomorrow, and every day of our existence—a variable that will never stop changing.

A lady said she doesn't believe God's purpose for her life still holds because of the things she has done with her life. I looked into her eyes and told her nothing could change God's mind concerning His purpose for her life. The detours we have experienced in the past, present, and future cannot and will not change God's purpose for our lives, except if we admit they can and also hold on to the lies of the Devil that the damage we have done to ourselves is beyond repair. The good news is that there is no fracture, disease, or addiction that the blood of Jesus cannot wash away. Our purpose is eternally consistent with God's essence. Our potential serves as a tool that would assist us in being dynamic, not just in what we do but also in who we are.

Gifts and Purpose

SIMILARLY TO POTENTIAL, gifts can be considered innate talents. God can work through us to carry out a specific assignment or set of activities. The innate capacity to perform particular tasks is known as a gift. God's capacity in us is confined to a unique or distinctive power that gives people a mental picture of who we are. Therefore, it is easy for me to recognise a proficient man playing the piano, and it is easy for me to characterise or label him a pianist since I see him display exceptional power in playing the piano.

The reality is that he possesses an innate capability of performing a function, and the essence of his gift lies in this potential. However, labelling him as a pianist might not accurately represent the purpose or motivation behind the gift given to him. Gifts cannot be fulfilled or taught; they are always stuck within us and can only be developed. Every time we perform to the best of our abilities, our gift is influenced and thus improved. Maximising our potential (God's ability to do all He can through us) improves the deployment capability of our gifts.

Purpose, on the other hand, determines the use of our gifts. This is true because whatever impact our gift has on humanity in the Spirit (nature) of righteousness and holiness is our purpose. If the outcome of our gift gives God glory, then our purpose is fulfilled. It is critical to understand that our talent is the source of our worth and value and that it will greatly benefit us if we skill up our gifts with discipline and godly character. Discipline sharpens our gifts, whereas godly character sustains the access and relationships that allow us to utilise our gifts.

Career and Purpose

A CAREER DOES not always represent an individual's identity. A career is a field of human endeavour in which a person chooses to dominate and direct. It is solely a method of exchanging ideas to create wealth. Because of this, talented people tend to be the ones who have the most success in their chosen field. Your career depends on your gifts (values); most of the time, such gifts are not innate but obtained through education.

Purpose is who we are, and the gifts that enable us to accomplish our purpose are innate. In contrast to careers, purpose does not use retirement as a method of exiting our jobs. You can switch jobs anytime, but remember what the Manufacturer had in mind when He formed you; you can not change His intentions for your life. Do you feel like there is no meaning to your life? Ask the Lord to reveal His plans and purpose for your life to you. This revelation is a good option if you need help differentiating between your purpose and career. And if you feel like you don't have a career and are practically depressed because of it, the good news is that you can turn your purpose into a career.

Regardless of your chosen career, you can still fulfil God's purpose. There is a God's dimension in you that resonates with your career, and that dimension is what stands you out among your colleagues at work. This dimension is captured in the everyday instructions you receive from the Lord and obey. Your career is now giving you a platform to fulfil His will, and it is not a thing of shame. You only fulfil your role as God's masterpiece created for His wonders. Your career becomes your pulpit for ministry.

In summary, the purpose is to be who we are as predetermined by God. It is God's preordained outcome for our lives. Our potential is God's endless power to fulfil any endeavour. Our gift is God's intrinsic capacity to accomplish specific functions, which is the source of our worth. Our profession is what we do, not necessarily who we are. It is essential to remember that potentials, gifts, and careers are all means to an end. God's goal is the end. Our potential and gifts can be used for a variety of purposes, but God gave us His abilities and gifts to help us serve His purposes.

Chapter Four

CHRIST, OUR MODEL

Luke 4:18-19

> *The Spirit of the Lord [is] upon Me because He has anointed Me [the Anointed One, the Messiah] to preach the good news [the gospel] to the poor; He has sent Me to announce release to the captives and recovery of sight to the blind; to send forth as delivered those who are oppressed [who are downtrodden, bruised, crushed, and broken down by calamity]; to proclaim the accepted and acceptable year of the Lord [the day when salvation and the free favours of God profusely abound].*

This describes the purpose of our Lord Jesus. The truth is that Jesus was not just speaking to people who were oppressed in His days when He made this statement; He was also referring to all those who would come to believe in His name and the anointing from generation to generation. Our Lord Jesus' primary purpose was to reconcile humanity to God through His death and resurrection. As opposed to us, He is a perfect image of the Father; hence, He does not need to conform to the likeness of God. By His shed blood, He—who did not know sin—gave us the ability to triumph over both sin and death and we, who had been dead in sin, were given eternal life. This eternal life allows us to carry out Jesus' mission, as stated in Luke 4:18–19.This verse indicates that Christ wants to accomplish His goals as we conform to Him daily. Everyone who has received the gift of salvation and acknowledged Christ as their Lord must carry out Christ's purpose in their endeavours. All of God's investments in us (His potential, gifts, anointing, spiritual blessings, and monetary rewards) are intended to help us carry out the mission of Christ. This is the ultimate purpose of our Lord Jesus, which He still fulfils even now through the Holy Spirit and His vessels.

Let's go back to Jesus' mission statement.

He has anointed me to preach the gospel:

We have been anointed and consecrated to perform different functions in the body of Christ. Just as our body has different parts that cannot be substituted for one another, so are our functionalities in the body of Christ.

The lungs will not do what the kidneys do, and the nose will not do what the mouth does. Although they belong to the same body, the body's functionality is determined by the supply of each part, without feeling superiority over the other. Everything you do in your role contributes to the overall mission of Christ's earthly ministry. This anointing distinguished you and gave you the authority to carry out your duties. Knowing what I have been designated for is crucial. Life's problems can enchant or seduce us to the point that we risk becoming soiled.

Not only adultery and fornication have the potential to pollute us. If we are truly born of the Spirit, as Apostle Paul warned us, fornication and adultery should not be brought up among us. Therefore, I am not referring to contamination caused by what we do to our bodies but rather by what we do to our souls (inordinate affection, quest for fame and popularity, mammon, personal ambition, and the like).

By His Grace, some of us are aware of our assignments, but we are dissatisfied with what we have been given. We believe our task won't make us famous, so we are jealous of another man's assignment. This is the Spirit of seduction from the pit of hell. Worldliness is actively fighting a mental battle with us. Every time we follow the crowd, we reject Christ. Living for what Christ lives for is what we are meant to do. And if we must live for what He did, we should be dedicated to Him and grafted into His body to live His life and carry out His mission.

1 John 2:26–27

> *These things have I written unto you concerning them that seduce you, but the anointing you have received from Him abides in you, and you need not that any man teach you. Still, as the same anointing teaches you of all things, is truth and is no lie, you shall abide in Him even as it has taught you.*

The anointing is God's ability in us. These abilities gain expression as He teaches and helps us to abide in Him. The anointing manifests itself in diverse ways (gifts) through us when we submit to Him. The anointing helps us to know and stick to our tasks as we follow the Holy Spirit's guidance and instruction. This is how we can eliminate any division-causing traits that have crept into the body of Christ, such as covetousness, hatred, and jealousy.We have deviated from what the anointing taught us, and some people are not satisfied with their calling because they feel it is not making them known. Everyone wants to be an apostle nowadays because they appear to be more popular. You and I are first set apart for the Lord and then assigned to different parts of His body to carry out His purposes on earth. Know this, and enjoy your freedom.Preaching the gospel should be the first goal of our consecration. Speaking of the gospel, there are many practices in our society today that claim to be the gospel. Some even claim that the time we live in influences God's will. Others claim that the period we live in impacts God's will. As a result, how the gospel is communicated and what the gospel is have changed to fit this or their generation better. Despite appearing to be the truth, it lacks Christ, the essence of the truth.

One of Satan's defamatory seduction techniques is to tell them what appeals to their emotions and reasoning but is harmful, discrediting the truth. The gospel remains the gospel. It cannot be improved or modernised. The means of communicating or preaching the gospel are still the same for anyone who cares to receive it. The gospel is received through the salvation Jesus offers when we believe in His death and resurrection. Beyond confessing Christ as our Lord and Saviour, this gift of salvation leaves us responsible for taking a complete u-turn from our unrighteous and wicked ways (repentance). When we do this, we have received it; it is about Christ and nothing else.The gospel is to proclaim and declare the rule and dominion of Christ not just with our mouths but, more importantly, with our lives, the things that pertain to salvation and godly living. This is the power of God at work first in us, with evidence or proof that His power is truly at work in us. The gospel is the proclamation, a public show, of the Kingdom of God, the reign of His righteousness, peace, and joy in the Holy Spirit through our words and conduct in our private and public lives. These are not platitudes or cliches; they are facts everyone can feel and see. It is a life that the Holy Spirit has empowered.

The life our Lord Jesus would live if He were to be in this world is the gospel. The gospel is the personality of Christ that must be experienced and lived. Our lives must transmit so much power, so we were set apart. Anointed to become a transformer who can transform lives and situations, including those around us, through the power of the Holy Spirit who lives in us; the gospel is Christ, the power and wisdom of God. This is what believers are. We are His witnesses, proof of His power and wisdom through our conduct and lifestyle.

Only the sons of perdition will not be transformed by the gospel. Whatever your part accomplishes, it is all part of the bigger picture of Christ's mission on earth. This anointing did not just set you apart but also gave you the required power to administer your office. It is very critical to know what I have been set apart for. There are issues with life romancing or seducing us to the point that we may be defiled.

To preach the gospel to the poor:

Every mission statement has a target audience. In the case of our Lord Jesus, He was sent to the poor. If God's kingdom must be established on earth, poverty must be dealt with from the root. It is not a lack of money or material blessings in this context. There is a need for more spiritual currency. That blood is the exchange for enduring wealth and success. There are people in our workplace and associations who are rich in the things of this world but are spiritually bankrupt, vulnerable, helpless, and powerless to accomplish or fulfil God's purpose for their lives. Lowly or destitute of Christlike virtues and eternal riches and have not tasted God's power. These are the people Jesus called the poor.

As believers, our assignment is to these groups of people in our society. We are obligated to proclaim the gospel to the poor. This declaration is not just in words but in our conduct and lifestyle. Christ is the good news, and we must transmit His life to those destitute of godly character or virtues. The Holy Spirit is the transformer, but we are the devices or vessels through which the transformation power of the Holy Spirit flows into the world around us. Let the light of peace, righteousness, and joy in the Holy Spirit shine into people in our workplace, family, and associations. This mission is one we all, as followers of Christ, must fulfil. It is the ultimate purpose of God for our lives.

To announce release to the captive:

Captivity is the consequence of spiritual bankruptcy. Diseases and various infirmities, debt, demonic oppression, all forms of delay, and addictions (to drugs, immorality, food, etc.) have all held many people captive. The captives are those who are under Satan's dominion and whose brains have fallen into his hands. The captives are prisoners of war. This explains ancestral courses' validity and legal grounds for those who have not given their lives to Christ. We have been set apart and anointed to establish the rule and reign of God's kingdom on earth.

Our consecration empowered us to release all who have become captives of the world system (the kingdom of darkness). If every believer is indeed preaching the gospel and our lives are demonstrating the power of God, there will be no captives in our churches today, and that makes it a point of duty to reach out to the world around us with the same light we have that destroys all forms of captivity. Our workplace, community, and neighbourhood become our mission fields to show forth His power and might through us so that every knee will bow and tongues will confess that He is the Lord over all things.

Every profession and field of learning is trying to give humanity freedom. With all the improvements in health care delivery, motivational talks from idealists, laws and policies from social scientists, advancements in science and technology, financial literacy, and skill acquisitions, the universe has yet to experience absolute peace. All the systems have repeatedly failed because they are all products of good and evil. The world will get darker by the day until the sons of righteousness (believers) arise to our calling by the election of grace.Righteousness, not technology, is what elevates every nation. Every invention of man has subjected him to more oppression than the liberation he envisaged. These inventions are either made by some powers or hijacked by these same powers just for them to be in charge.

The world is in a dilemma, and this calls for the rising of the sons of God to release the captives of the so-called mighty of this world. Every solution, propounded by the intelligence of men, only lasts for a short time and further subjects him to slavery or captivity. This is the reason Satan is fighting the gospel, but the good news is that the Spirit and the anointing of the Lord are upon us to release the captives. This is our collective assignment.

Let believers arise and go into all the sectors of governance and industries and declare war against the oppressor, resisting him continually. Announce the release of the captive. The two-edged sword to fight this war is the word of God, not just in our mouths but in our hearts, conduct, and lifestyle. We must also be fervent in the place of prayer, which is where authority is delegated to us. This is the Jubilee. Jubilee is the declaration of war against all that has held the creation in captivity or bondage. This is Joy. It is the Kingdom of God. The Holy Ghost is the dunamis (power) that produces freedom. Freedom triggered joy.

That is why it is called joy in the Holy Ghost. It will be taboo to carry the Holy Ghost and still be oppressed.

The oppressor has to be bound for the captive to be set free. The oppressor will be bound when we walk in the light of Jesus (the word of God). The captive who has been set free must enrol in the discipleship class to be taught of the Lord and walk in the footprints of Jesus. This is a discipleship or mentorship programme. Talking about mentorship, let me appeal to mentors and coaches to be careful not to prioritise money over souls. Most of the things we have packaged for our master classes and monetised are what we learned when discipleship classes were what they should be.

Recovery of sight to the blind:

When discussing the recovery of sight, observing the miracles throughout the Old Testament before the public ministry of our Lord Jesus is essential. We will discover that the opening of sight begins with Christ. Are there not blind people in the days of the prophets before Christ? There were about eight instances of Jesus opening the eyes of blind people in the New Testament. (Matthew 9:27–31, Mardkk 8:22–26, Matthew 12:22–23, Luke 18:35–43, Mark 10:46–52, John 9:1-41, Matthew 15:29–31, Matthew 21:14). The significance of this miracle is to prove to the entire human race that only Jesus has power over darkness. He is the light that darkness cannot comprehend. Jesus is the true light that gives light to everyone coming into this world.

The scripture made us understand that this light that gives light to all men is in the life of Christ. Everyone who has received the life of Christ has also received His light. This life imposes the obligation to care for the blind—those who lack the life that generates the light that gives all men sight.

The Holy Spirit will lead us to those who need sight. Just as He led our Lord Jesus, darkness is the sole cause of captivity, and darkness will continue to run its course until there is illumination.

As representatives of Christ, we must illuminate our sectors, nations, and territories. It is our understanding of God that produces godly virtues that illuminate the darkness around us. The soul that is destitute of Christ-like character will be subjected to all kinds of oppression as a result of mental blindness, ignorance, loss of identity, and pride. The only path that the devil works on unhindered is the path engrossed in darkness (ignorance) and rides on this path into people's minds and souls to control (dominion) their perceptions, thoughts, passions, cravings, appetites, emotions, purpose, and intellect.

I call our attention to the truth of God's word: we are obligated to open the eyes of the blind and give sight (impartation) to those who have lost their sight (direction and purpose). A young believer can study the scriptures under the guidance of the Holy Spirit and grow, but that cannot substitute for discipleship because of the leverage discipleship offers. Opening or recovering sight is not a one-off encounter. It is a continuous exercise in renewing one's mind through the word of God and prayer. In one of the discipleship classes, Jesus asked them:

Matthew 6:23

> *But if your eyes are unsound, your whole body will be full of darkness. If then the very light in you (your conscience) is darkened, how dense is that darkness?*

The oppressed, who are now free, must be schooled in the school of the Spirit. Taught by Him, possess His mind, be baptised by His Spirit, and be filled with the Holy Spirit. The implication of Jesus' mission statement is to see our assignment in this light. He has shown us the strategy and road map, and we must follow Jesus' mission. Whatever part of His body He called us to be must reflect Jesus' statement of purpose. We are wired differently to be able to affect the world system holistically with Jesus' mission; whichever sector our gifts fit in, the mission is the same. Jesus says that our conduct should inspire and give light (vision) to those who live in darkness.

Send forth to deliver those who are oppressed:

Christ did not only want to deliver; He also wanted to set free the oppressed. By the election of Grace, He intends to send forth those who have been delivered.

This freedom is subject to control by Grace. Freedom without control will only promote anarchy and abuse. This freedom comes with responsibilities. The delivered person must respond to the grace of God that brought them liberty. Christ is the world's saviour, and He intends to raise saviours like Him who will go into all sectors of human endeavours and proclaim the good news. Our response to grace—God's ability—makes us save others, too. These saviours are born of the Spirit, establishing the purposes of God everywhere they go. Those delivered by the Master received their sight and were also sent forth to fill their domain and territory with the knowledge and glory of God as water covers the sea (Habakkuk 2:14).

We are to proclaim the acceptable year of the Lord:

This is a proclamation of grace, not as liberty to continue in sin but as an instrument of power to fulfil the purposes of God. Jesus' mission must be our mission. As Christ was in this world, so are we. Only those who have experienced salvation can explore faith in God. God's power is released from glory to glory through our faith in God and the election of Grace. This is our core assignment on earth. God's kingdom is only established on earth to the degree of the population of the poor, oppressed, blind, and captives that we have in our workplace, neighbourhood, community, state, and nation. The fewer oppressed people around us, the more of God's rule and kingdom there are in our world.

I speak to you today with the authority of God's word, "Arise and shine, for your light (salvation and deliverance) has come, and the glory of the Lord rises upon you." The earnest expectation of the entire God's creation is eagerly waiting for your manifestation. Salvation supplies us with God's Grace (His ability and life) to live as He lived, living the life He laid down for us. If I must not lose the joy of salvation, I must continually live in Him, move in Him (taking order from Him through the Holy Spirit), and have my being (my essence, relevance, and satisfaction) in Him.

Galatians 2:20

> *"I have been crucified with Christ; it is no longer I who live, but Christ lives in me. The life that I now live in the flesh is lived by faith in the Son of God, who loved me and gave Himself for me."*

Chapter Five

PURPOSE AND PRAYER

James 5:16

> *Confess to one another, therefore, your faults (your slips, your false steps, your offences, your sins), and pray [also] for one another, that you may be healed and restored [to a spiritual tone of mind and heart]. A righteous man's earnest (heartfelt, continued) prayer makes tremendous power available [dynamic in its working].*

We have established that the soul's salvation should be the quest of everyone who longs to see the purposes of God fulfilled in their lives and that Jesus is the way, the truth, and the life. A life without Jesus will only wander in the jungle of life all through its stay on earth and have no hope for eternity with Christ. The scripture we just read gave us a clear perspective on what makes prayer work.The first principle is the principle of repositioning our souls. This principle addresses the need to deal with sin and not hinder our prayers. Confess your sins and repent so your soul can be healed and restored to a spiritual tone (aligning the frequency of minds, thoughts, and hearts with God's heart).

The second principle of effective and efficient prayer is continually praying. The repositioning of our mind and prayer persistence must be consistently observed to generate dynamic power in its approach to situations and circumstances.

The significance of prayer in a purpose-driven life is not negotiable. Our lives are an untold story of God's plan for the continuity of His work on earth through us (God's image and character). Prayer is one of those ways God communicates His plans to us. The execution and success of God's plan for our lives are predicated on effective, heartfelt, and continued prayer.A classic example is the birth of our Lord Jesus Christ. Long ago, before His birth, God's plan was revealed concerning the coming of the Messiah, the world's saviour, whose death and resurrection would reconcile man back to God. This plan was first revealed in Genesis 3:15, and scriptures or prophecies in the Old Testament mention His birth. Just to name a few (Isaiah 9:6, Isaiah 7:14, Isaiah 61:1, Micah 5:2, Hosea 11:1, Jeremiah 23:5, Jeremiah 31:15, Isaiah 42:1-4). These prophecies were not all fulfilled in the Old Testament. According to Bible theologians, between the Old Testament and the New Testament, God did not communicate with His people for approximately 400–600 years. The New Testament began with a beacon of hope through Anna and Simeon.

The Bible records that they continually prayed and fasted to fulfil all the prophecies about Christ. Every success in any human endeavour is a function of effective prayer. Even those in the kingdom of darkness do not hide their confidence in the deity they worship, thereby praying to their gods. Their allegiance is to Lucifer, and they are not apologetic about it. Prayer consecrates us to God, and consistent and persistent prayers help us accomplish God's purpose for our lives. Knowing God's purpose for our lives is spiritual, and we can not be carnal if we desire to fulfil God's purpose for our lives.

Sensuality limits us to our intuitiveness and intellect, which cannot decode the essence of our lives according to God's design. The scriptures give us a series of accounts of Jesus' prayer. One would have thought that our Lord Jesus would not have needed to pray to fulfil His mandate of reconciling humanity back to God. After all, Christ is the second person of the trinity; He is God, and why should God be praying to God?

To answer this question, we must understand that our Lord Jesus was a complete human with the capacity to be tempted, influenced, emotional, and all the other attributes of a human, just like you and me. Therefore, prayer becomes a channel through which He can constantly connect Himself to the Father, realign His will to His Father's will, be empowered, and quicken or strengthen Himself to stay on course for His purpose on earth. The account of Christ being led to the wilderness to pray and fast for forty days and nights validates prayer as a necessary instrument or device that helps us navigate the journey of our purpose on earth. Prayer prepares us for the future while also repositioning us for the present.

Purpose, Prayer, and the Anointing

PURPOSE IS GLAMOROUS when we embrace it and are willing to give it all it requires. Purpose itself is not what we do but who we are. Even though what we do can sometimes be interpreted as who we are, this reminds us that we sometimes mistake our gifts for our purpose. Many of us are known for our gifts but not for our purpose. Our gifts present us with the platform to manifest our purpose.

The effective use of our gifts is not only determined by the function of the gifts but rather by our purpose. And if we desire to be efficient with our gifts in helping to fulfil our purpose, we must recognise the role of the anointing. The anointing perfectly blends our gifts and

God's purpose for our lives. The anointing is God's empowerment on a vessel that prepares him for a particular task. Gifts are good, but they have limitations. The anointing interacts with the vessel (you) and is not merely a gift. The anointing represents God's dimension in the use of our gifts. For instance, everyone can sing regardless of their voice textures, but not all are anointed to sing. The fact that we all can talk and engage people in conversations doesn't mean we are all anointed to teach. When we experience ability beyond our capacity, the anointing is at work.

Acts 10:38 (AMP)

> *How God anointed and consecrated Jesus of Nazareth with the [Holy] Spirit and with strength, ability, and power; how He went about doing good and, in particular, curing all who were harassed and oppressed by [the power of] the devil, for God was with Him.*

Here, we see the anointing as the Holy Spirit manifesting Himself as the strength, power, and ability of God in the lives of God's people. The whole essence of the anointing is to consecrate us and set us apart as a special vessel created to show God's glory, wisdom, and power in our specific assignments.

Prayer, on the other hand, is the life of the anointed. Our Lord Jesus is the perfect example of this truth.

Luke 5:16 (NLT)

But Jesus often withdrew to the wilderness for prayer.

Mark 1:35 (AMP)

And in the morning, long before daylight, He got up and went out to a deserted place, and there He prayed.

Luke 6:12-13 (AMP)

Now, in those days, it occurred that He went up into a mountain to pray and spent the whole night in prayer to God. And when it was day, He summoned His disciples and selected from them twelve, whom He named apostles [special messengers].

The above scriptures give us the accounts of Jesus' prayer. Imagine God (Christ) praying all through the night. These scriptures help us to understand that prayer is the essential ingredient for fulfilling God's purpose and it is important to mention that every significant milestone of our Lord Jesus' ministry was preceded by a long, compelling, and fervent prayer. Jesus did not just go about doing good; He went about doing what He saw His Father doing. As we remain consistent and steadfast in prayer, we increase our consecration because the more time we spend with God in prayer and study of His word, the more consecrated we become to doing more for Him.

We need to remember that we can lose the anointing not because God took it away from us but because we fail to engage the anointing with the things that supply life to the anointing. So, the anointing begins to lose functionality due to a lack of prayer. The anointing can be depleted or completely lost if it is deprived of the life required to power it. God anointed Christ to fulfil God's mandate for His life, but He still had to pray earnestly to see His mission fulfilled, so we must pray fervently to see the purposes of God for our lives come through.

1 John 2:27

> *"But the anointing which you have received from Him abides in you, and you do not need that anyone teach you; but as the same anointing teaches you concerning all things, as it is true and is not a lie, and just as it has taught you, you will abide in Him."*

God's anointing teaches us everything concerning us, including our calling and assignment. Prayer creates the right atmosphere for the anointing to function at full capacity. Prayer keeps our minds on God's ability (power) within us to do His will and abide in His anointing (His grace). We need more than just the omnipresence of God to follow His instructions and fulfil our purpose. We need to abide in His presence through prayer to experience His manifest presence, which will put us in charge through the demonstration of His power in us and through us. The world awaits the manifest presence of God in us, whom He has redeemed by His blood and set apart for His glory.

We must understand that His manifest presence comes through vessels that carry the abiding presence of Yahweh. The challenge we often face is that we think that because we have good intentions—renewing the earth and knowing God's plans and how they would be executed—that's all there is. Jesus also had all these, but He was still led to pray. It is not enough to have good intentions or know God's will and His plans, but rather to tarry in His presence to receive a sizable quantum of energy commensurate with the light (the task we were given) we are called to show forth. Your purpose, assignment, good deeds, and intentions are nothing but ideas. Not all ideas materialise into substances that are evident in nature or the cosmos.

2 Thessalonians 1:11 (MSG)

> *Because we know that this extraordinary day is just ahead, we pray for you all the time—pray that our God will make you fit for what he's called you to be; pray that he'll fill your good ideas and acts of faith with his energy so that it all amounts to something.*

This scripture says that your good ideas, dreams, visions, and plans need the energy of God to leave the realm of ideas or thoughts and enter the realm of reality. God's purposes for our lives are eternal, and God will not change His mind concerning what He has for us, but we need to understand that His purposes can be stopped or hindered when we are not praying fervently. We are not praying to change God or His intentions concerning us. We are rather praying to accept His sovereignty over our situation. By doing so, we are becoming not just His image but His hands, through which His purposes are done on earth.

What our mortal bodies can do is limited without fervent prayer. God is God, and He does whatever pleases Him. Accepting what pleases God is how we become. The purpose of our prayers is to find alignment with God. I remember when I was looking for a job shortly after my one-year compulsory service to my nation. I realised that I could not articulate exactly what I should be doing while waiting for my dream job, but the Holy Spirit kept leading me to the scriptures, and I found it fulfilling to pray those scriptures.Today, I see those scriptures becoming my reality. Years later, I discovered that all God wanted from me was to align my desires with His. Prayer helps us build up our faith in God. It is a proof of our absolute dependence on God. Prayer is a journey that must be progressive, and the progressiveness is predicated on consistency. Sometimes, it is challenging to believe that prayer works effectively because our senses have already figured out all the possible plans for a successful life. The world is also moving so fast that the word 'wait' is no longer tolerated, compounded by the fact that there are numerous quick fixes available that appear to provide us with success. The truth is that we usually achieve success but lack the wisdom that produces fulfilment.

Many place more priority on other kinds of strategies than prayer. Strategies without prayer are like having a new automobile without fuel to power the engine. Prayer is the vehicle and medium through which grace is consistently supplied. The secret of true greatness is understanding God's purpose for our lives. What is made manifest was once revealed. If it is not revealed, it will not manifest.

Amos 3:7

> *"Indeed, the sovereign Lord never does anything until he reveals His plans to His servant, the prophet."*

Many people today live a confused life simply because they never sought the face of God through prayer to know God's plan for their lives. Please note that it has to be revealed for it to manifest. There is something in the mind of God that beckons for establishment in this realm; only men who have found alignment or whose desire is that which is in the mind of God will establish God's kingdom on earth.

Matthew 6:10

> *May your kingdom come soon. May your will be done on earth as it is in heaven.*

God's purposes are birthed on the altar of prayer. God's purpose is the seed for your conception. It started and was conceived in the mind of God. Let's see what God told the prophet Jeremiah in the first chapter of the book of Jeremiah, verse five. *"I knew you before I formed you in your mother's womb. Before you were born, I set you apart and appointed you as my prophet to the nations."* God told the children of Israel in Babylon through Prophet Jeremiah in the twenty-nineth chapter of the book of Jeremiah, verse 11: *"For I know the plans I have for you, "says the Lord. "They are planned for good and not for disaster, to give you a future and hope."*

If we combine these two scriptures, we will discover that our existence is preordained because of its essence—God's thought. We are not born for disaster; our birth was not accidental. The scripture says it was not an accident, even if you were born physically out of wedlock. You are not a misfit, nor is your existence a misconstrued part of creation. Our existence was preordained, planned, and well-thought-out by God.

How does this relate to prayer? The last statement in Jeremiah twenty-nine, verse five, says, "*to give you a future and a hope.*" Some translations say there is a future and an expected end. Looking at this statement, we will realise that our future is God's past. Therefore, our present must begin with God, who already has the script for that expected end. Remember, the expected end is not our expected end or expectations but God's expectations for our lives. So, we must begin with God. There is this popular quote by Dr. Myles Munroe, Blessed Memory. He said, "**If you want to know the purpose of a thing, do not ask the thing; do ask the manufacturer.**" A microphone cannot tell you its purpose; only the manufacturer can. So, you and I cannot tell us why we are on earth; only God can.

No amount of brainstorming, reasoning, artificial intelligence, or intellectual capacity can reveal our purpose. It begins with a thought in the mind of God; He then speaks us forth into existence to fulfil His intentions.

Revelation 4:11

> *"Worthy are you, our Lord and God, to receive glory, honour, and power, for you created all things, and by your will they existed and were created."*

Prayer is the channel through which God's reasoning is revealed to us. When we seek the face of God in prayer, He will reveal our purposes—our core assignment—to us. David, the psalmist, understood this when he said to God in Psalm 139:15,

> *"My substance was not hidden from you when I was made in secret and curiously wrought in the lowest parts of the earth."*

The word substance in that scripture means strength, body, or frame. Your purpose is your strength, frame, essence, or body. In secondary school, when we were taught how to write an essay, I discovered that one thing common to all types of essays is that they all have three components: an introduction, a body, and a conclusion. The bulk of the essay is in the body. Even though the introduction tells you the purpose of the essay, the details of that purpose are written in the body. David said that his strength might be hidden from him but not from God. The details of his life are with and in God.

The purpose is spiritual. It is the glory within. Just as faith is the substance of things hoped for or the evidence of things not seen (Hebrews 11:1), so is our purpose. Our purpose is God's expected end—thought and reasoning. Our purpose is the outcome of our lives, which God has already decided. We receive it by faith and run with it. I pray that God will impact the discipline of prayer on us so that we will not only know God's purpose for our lives but also fulfil it.

Chapter Six

PURPOSE AND INFLUENCE

It is honourable for our God to see us work according to His will and purposes. This gesture of honour is significant to God's redemption plan for saving the world around us. There is a hope of glory for this generation—Christ in us. Christ is not just our hope of glory; His life in us is an unapologetic expression of His nature, and His essence is the hope of glory for the world. He exchanged our filthiness with His righteousness, which repositioned us to behold His face, doing His bindings (righteous acts) not in our strength but by His Grace and the empowerment of His Spirit.

Growing up as teenagers, we sang a song that said, "The world is a market, and heaven is home." This song did something to my mind, and I became unconscious about what I do. I lost an integral part of God's righteousness that beckons me to take responsibility for His righteousness by ensuring that I am in complete alignment with His will for my life. I was trying to be holy, forgetting that to be holy is to be one with God in every matter.

For instance, God is light, and nothing can change that. Exhibiting His light (nature) is what makes me holy.

I found the truth as I grew in my knowledge of His word. It shows me that my relevance on earth is much needed since heaven is a resting place. I discovered the word of Christ that says, "Occupy till I come." I realised that when my righteousness is allowed to reflect God's righteousness, it will become a sceptre of authority and power rather than filthy rags.

Psalm 45:6–7

Your throne, O God, is forever and ever; the sceptre of righteousness is the sceptre of Your kingdom. You love righteousness, uprightness, and right standing with God and hate wickedness; therefore, God, Your God, has anointed You with the oil of gladness above Your fellows. (AMP)
Your throne, O God, endures forever and ever. Your royal power is expressed in justice. You love

> *what is right and hate what is wrong. Therefore, God, your God, has anointed you, pouring out the oil of joy on you more than on anyone else. (NLT)*

I was once blind, but now I see. I have received His light into my heart; I have the mind of God, and I share the same perspectives with God on His intentions for the earth He created. If the sceptre of righteousness is the sceptre of His kingdom, more righteous people are needed to enforce His reign. Someone is saying, "I think we are talking about God's kingdom here; why do we need to enforce it?" Righteous people are God's kingdom enforcers. They refuse to compromise their allegiance and loyalty to the King, so they rely on God's justice system. There is a need for these people.

The scriptures say the harvest is ready, but the harvesters are few. I know it is more than enough when a man single-handedly takes his stand against corruption in his workplace, but think about having ten or more of such men stand their ground against unrighteous acts in the same office. I believe the impact will not be the same.

The more righteous people we see in a sector, a nation, or any gathering, the more His glory we see. Friends, it is not just a cliche that "we were saved to save others." We were saved to live the very life of Jesus beyond the four walls of our fellowships, churches, and families. The creation is waiting for the manifestation of saviours—

those who have received the life of the Master—and their lives (gains and losses) do not matter to them because they are dead to themselves but alive in Christ. This is the ultimate purpose of the death and resurrection of our Lord Jesus Christ. There is a life that brings peace to every situation.

There is a quality of life that can transform an entire race or society. No carnal man has this kind of life. Even intelligence and advancements in social behaviour and technology lack the quality of this life that produces true transformation. This life is only found in Christ, our Lord and Saviour. He gave His life so that we could live, do His will, and illuminate the world with His light, wisdom, and glory. He called us out of darkness—ignorance, poverty, obscurity, and abusive interactions with the world—and into His light. We, despite our insignificance, have emerged as agents of transformation.

1 Peter.2:9 (MSB)

> *But you are the ones chosen by God, chosen for the high calling of priestly work, chosen to be a holy people, God's instruments to do his work and speak out for him, to tell others of the night-and-day difference he made for you.*

The time has come for us to take our faith in God beyond just meeting our needs and binding and casting out demons. The real test of our faith in God comes when we stand for righteousness, peace, and justice.

What our faith says in the face of persecution and trials shows whether our allegiance is to God. There are two types of believers that I have seen in the course of my interactions with church folks. The first category is those who believe that this world is not their own and that they are just passing by. These believers are very laid-back. They cannot hurt a fly and are just mindful of going to heaven, not moved by the state of things on earth. Their understanding of eternal life is heaven. They are not interested in expanding the frontiers of God's kingdom on earth. I think we've a couple of these kinds of believers in our neighbourhood.

The second category is believers who strongly believe that the only proof of their readiness for the Lord's coming is to occupy the earth, showing forth the fruit of righteousness, fulfilling God's designs for their lives, and increasing the frontiers of God's kingdom. They believe the earth is the Lord and are busy cultivating it, tilling their domain of influence with God's gifts, and living each day as if it is all they have gotten.

These groups of believers are practically in all sectors, from political to social to economic to civil service. The only challenge is that this group of believers have only succeeded in bringing the produce of their gifts and their diligence to work as tithes and offerings to the Lord. Don't get me wrong; there is nothing wrong with paying tithes and giving an offering to the Lord. I am only saying that God deserves more and expects more from us than monetary sacrifice. David said this in one of His meditations in Psalm.

<u>Psalm 40:6–10</u>

> *"That You take no delight in sacrifices or offerings. Now that you have made me listen, I finally understand, You don't require burnt offerings or sin offerings."*
> *Then I said, "Look, I have come. And this has been written about me in your scroll: I take joy in doing your will, my God, for your law is written on my heart." I have told all your people about your justice. I have not been afraid to speak out, as you, O Lord, well know. I have not kept this good news hidden in my heart; I have talked about your faithfulness and saving power. I have told everyone in the great assembly of your unfailing love and faithfulness".*

Friends, it is okay to talk about righteousness, preach to ourselves with deep revelations from God's word in church, and organise word conferences and worship events. Still, we must remember that the purpose of those events and activities is to become like Christ. Therefore, if those activities are not fulfilling this singular purpose, then it means that we are not different from noisemakers and socialites on the streets. When purpose is known, it must influence circumstances and everything around it.

Fulfilling God's purpose requires denying oneself what appears to be a gain and counting it as a loss. If sleeping with my boss for one-night results in a promotion, financial stability, complete control over my workplace, or any form of compromise on my faith and intimacy with God, it will be difficult for me to consider it a loss. Knowing that we do not fulfil God's will on our own terms is crucial. God's purposes are fulfilled in His terms. The clay cannot dictate to the potter how it should be moulded.

Elements of Kingdom Influence

THE WORD INFLUENCE, according to the Advanced Offline Dictionary is defined as the bringing about of an effect, physical or moral, by a gradual process; controlling power quietly exerted; power or authority arising from the elevated station; excellence of character or intellect; wealth; reputation; the power of impelling or directing; credit weight of character.

Most of the time, influence is not violent but subtle and has an unseen force or power that is making the effect. There is an elevated position in which every believer in Christ operates, and situations and circumstances bow to the authority of that position.The scripture says in Ephesians 2:6 that "*God raised us with Christ and seated us with Him in the heavenly realms in Christ Jesus.*"This is our reality, and not exercising the authority and power of Christ in our space or sector will subject humanity to oppression and undue hardship. Permit me to share three major forces God constituted for our influence. According to the gospel of John, Chapter Fifteen, verse sixteen, Jesus said,

> *"You have not chosen Me, but I have chosen you, and I have appointed you [I have planted you], that you might go and bear fruit and keep on bearing, and that your fruit may be lasting [that it may remain, abide], so that whatever you ask the Father in My Name [as presenting all that I am], He may give it to you. This is what I command you: that you love one another."*

In this text, we see fruitfulness (physical growth, numerical growth, and spiritual growth) and love. The third force is in the account of Matthew, chapter twenty-eight, verses eighteen to twenty. Jesus said,

> *"Jesus approached and, breaking the silence, said to them, All authority (all power of rule) in heaven and on earth has been given to Me. Go then and make disciples of all the nations, baptising them into the name of the Father and of the Son and the Holy Spirit, teaching them to observe everything that I have commanded you, and behold, I am with you all the days [perpetually, uniformly, and on every occasion], to the [very] close and consummation of the age. Amen (so let it be)*

The emphasis on fruitfulness is evident in Matthew's account, as it was in John's account. These two accounts gave us the kingdom influence elements: fruitfulness, love, and teaching (education). Let us look into these elements. As I said earlier, these elements are forces that can break into any space or sector, and when they do, we see the kingdom of God established and unshakeable in those territories.

Fruitfulness

FRUITFULNESS MEANS AN increase. When our Lord Jesus says 'be fruitful', He means all-round fruitfulness (spiritual, physical, financial, material, and all). Fruitfulness is very necessary for influence. What one person will do is different from what two persons can do. The scriptures say, *"One will chase a thousand, and two will put ten thousand to a fight" Deuteronomy 32:30.* In other words, a believer of Christ can influence at least a thousand individuals; when we have two believers in a place, they stand to influence at least ten thousand people. This is the essence of God's commanded blessings of fruitfulness to man at creation. I know our increase as individuals or the body of Christ is not negotiable because it was not just a blessing but a commanded blessing. We need to be intentional and purposeful to enforce this blessing.

It will amaze you to know that every living creature has received the blessing of an increase from God.

Genesis 1:21- 22 (The birds and sea creatures)

God created the great sea monsters and every living creature that moves, which the waters brought forth abundantly, according to their kinds, and every winged bird according to its kind. And God saw that it was good (suitable, admirable), and He approved it. And God blessed them, saying, Be fruitful, multiply, and fill the waters in the seas, and let the fowl multiply in the earth.

Genesis 1:25 (NLT)

God made all sorts of wild animals, livestock, and small animals, each able to reproduce more of its kind. And God saw that it was good.

God is saying here that the only way creation will not go into extinction is by staying in their habitat (domain) and multiplying. Why increase? It is because their increase is tied to their relevance (purpose). Today, the world is going back to a state of voidness and darkness because there is an abuse of certain creatures that hinders their growth, distorts their influence, and has an impact on the environment, which is a direct beneficiary of their purpose and influence. Today, we are experiencing unusual climate change because the trees, the oceans, and their creatures have been robbed of their purpose and influence due to man's activities.

Genesis 1:26 -30

God said, Let Us [Father, Son, and Holy Spirit] make humanity in Our image, after Our likeness, and let them have complete authority over the fish of the sea, the birds of the air, the [tame] beasts, and over all of the earth, and over everything that creeps upon the earth. So God created man in His image; in the image and likeness of God, He created him; male and female, He created them.

And God blessed them and said to them, Be fruitful, multiply, and fill the earth, and subdue it [using all its vast resources in the service of God and man]; and have dominion over the fish of the sea, the birds of the air, and over every living creature that moves upon the earth. And God said, See, I have given you every plant yielding seed on the face of all the land and every tree with seed in its fruit; you shall have them for food. And to all the animals on the earth, every bird of the air, and everything that creeps on the ground - to everything in which there is the breath of life - I have given every green plant for food. And it was so.

We see again that man's influence is linked to his essence, and the continuation of that influence is dependent on God's ability in man to reproduce himself. Therefore, God commanded multiplication. This speaks to the population growth we see in the world today. However, there are human forces strategically positioned in the governments of nations that are routing for depopulation. They have depopulated the trees, sea creatures, and animals for their selfish gains, and now humans are their target.

They promote many theories and systems just to make us feel the increase in our population is a curse and not a blessing.

These individuals are nothing but agents of darkness, working hand in hand with their father, Lucifer. They fail to understand that God has pronounced His blessings on humanity, and His blessings are irreversible. Every nation will make continuous progress when the blessing of increase is properly harnessed. I know the world is heading to a place where a few people will completely be in control of all the sectors of the world. We have seen nations subscribing to every system and policy that will reduce the world population.

The main agenda of abortion policy, homosexuality, and the confusion relating to gender is population reduction. We have seen countries recently give statistics on the reduction in their population. Some individuals have taken hold of the world, and now the creation is eagerly waiting for the manifestations of the Sons of God (Romans 8:19). If you carefully read along with me, you will notice a contradiction in the world system's influence strategy. The world's government is advising men to reduce their numbers or risk losing their influence (essence), but the kingdom of God says, *"Multiply and subdue the earth, and the kingdom of this world will become the kingdom of our God and His sons" (Genesis 1:28).*

No matter what the world does, God is always ahead. The world can only abort physical pregnancy and dreams and aspirations, but She can't stop the purposes of God. God has commanded an increase, and His blessings are irrevocable. There is a system of conception the Lord is calling our attention to. The same gospel says, *"Be filled with God and set your affection on the things above, see what the Father sees and do His work while it is the day, for the evening time is drawing closer than when the day began." (Colossians 3:2).* When we conceive these words, there will be a rebirth of change catalysts that will contend with the enemy at the gates.

I want to call our attention to a fundamental truth about increase: growth is essential to increase. Fruitfulness entails maturity. I have never seen an infant or a child giving birth or nursing a baby; only adults do. There is a maturity level to attain for fruitfulness to be a reality. Therefore, fruitfulness begins with growth, which helps nurture the fruit we bear and see it mature. If we must take territories for Christ, we must mature in Christ and raise mature individuals who will continue to bear fruits just as we are.

God commanded us to increase because He knows the power and influence of a kingdom is a function of territories under her control. There is a need for us to extend our priesthood and kingship to every sector. God's kingdom of righteousness, peace, and joy in the Holy Ghost needs to be established. The deliverance of a nation is highly dependent on the population of the righteous in that nation.I will conclude on the need to populate the earth by showing us the order of operation God gave us in His word that guarantees influence. I don't know if we can recall a mathematical order of operation known as BODMAS. This order of operation is engaged whenever we want to solve a mathematical concept called FRACTION. Regarding having an unbroken influence in this world, Genesis 1 verse twenty-eight is the order of operation. God says," *be fruitful and multiply*". As much as we try to relate this to material prosperity and fruitfulness of the womb, we must not lose the rhema of this blessing.God made us in His image and likeness, and it was to that making that He commanded the blessing. God is saying we should reproduce and multiply His character and nature. So, this goes beyond natural birth or procreation. Our Lord Jesus also gave us the same commandment but related it to the reality of His time or days. He said, "*All authority (all power of rule) in heaven and on earth has been given to Me. Go then and make disciples of all the nations, baptising them into the name of the Father, Son, and Holy Spirit." (Matthew 28:18)*

You know it won't make any sense in Genesis if God said to the first man to go into the world and make disciples of all nations, but in the wisdom of God, He said to him, be fruitful. There are more disciples in the marketplace than in our church buildings. Today, what the church is experiencing is soul-recycling. We see folks leaving one denomination for another, looking for better networks or miracles. Nowadays, the church focuses more on buildings than people. God is telling us to replicate His character and nature in every nation of the world. The church, as a community of believers, is solely responsible for raising sons and not infants.

The second order of operation is to fill the earth. It takes righteous people to fill the earth with righteousness. God expects us to fill the earth with His glory, and these are the dimensions He has uniquely deposited in us, which is why man, as God's creation, will always be the solution to the world's crises. I remember talking to one of my mentees over the phone about glory. I told him God's glory is man's glory and vice versa. We came to this submission because he painted a scenario of the enemy stealing people's glory and making it look like the enemy is that powerful. The devil's greatest weapon is lies and sin in the life of anyone who claims to know God. The purpose of his lies is to manipulate and distort our thinking, and the purpose of sin is to separate us from God.

We have a misconception that the enemy stole our glory because we bought into his lies. We were deceived into believing the enemy took our glory on these grounds. But let us not be fooled any longer. The devil can not steal our glory, and it's time we make that clear and arise to shine forth God's Glory. Of course, separation from God is the departure of glory, and when we align our ways with God's ways, departed glory is restored. So, filling the earth is predicated on intimacy. We must admit that God's word cannot be fulfilled outside His presence, necessitating us to secure God's presence everywhere we go. People around us may not know or sense God's tangible presence, but we must. Just like every evil influence is powered by one demonic presence or the other, the positive influence must be powered by God's spirit.Therefore, life in the spirit is crucial to our influence on earth.

According to the first chapter of Genesis, verse twenty- eight, the last order is to subdue the earth. Man is meant to be in absolute control and management of the earth in accordance with God's purposes for everything He created. What can we say about the control of man on the earth today? Is it in alignment with God's original design? The answer is 'no'. Do not forget that man's control and management of the earth should bring about God's glory, covering the earth as waters cover the sea, but that is not the reality today. Man has lost his control system (God's Spirit and His reference); until he regains this loss, he cannot fulfil the commandment to subdue or dominate the earth.

I have discovered that the seed of dominion and the capacity to dominate are already in us. Still, sin or rebellion against God's instructions has reduced it to the survival instinct. We place survival over relevance, and things keep sliding backwards, falling out of divine order. The quest for survival opens us up to various vices, and we gradually become monsters rather than messiahs. The earth's potential will be under-utilised when we fail to fulfil God's dominion mandate at creation. There is no better way to influence our generation than the blessing of dominion. Managing the earth's resources to serve God and humanity following God's original intent is true dominion.

Teaching

Matthew 28:20

> *"Teaching them to observe everything that I have commanded you, and behold, I am with you all the days (perpetually, uniformly, and on every occasion), to the very close and consummation of the age." Amen (so let it be)*

IF WE MUST dominate our world and be in charge, we must understand and observe the teachings of our Lord Jesus Christ. We must teach and observe His commandments.

Isaiah 2:2-3 (NLT)

In the last days, the Temple of the Lord in Jerusalem will become the most important place on earth. People from all over the world will go there to worship. Many nations will come and say, "Come, let us go up to the mountain of the LORD, to the Temple of the God of Israel. He will teach us his ways there so that we may obey him." In those days, the LORD's teaching and word will go out from Jerusalem.

According to this scripture, a Christian is the most influential person on earth. God no longer dwells in temples; He lives in human vessels set apart to live holy just as He is Holy. The body of Christ has to fulfil Isaiah's prophecy. The only solution to the crises in our world today is to teach and observe all that Jesus commanded us to do. Jesus' commandments or teachings are never His ideas but God's will for humanity.

John 7:14-17

Then, midway through the festival, Jesus went up to the temple and began to teach. The Jewish leaders were surprised when they heard him. "How does he know so much when he hasn't studied everything we've studied?" they asked. So Jesus told them, "I'm not teaching my ideas, but those of God who sent me. Anyone who wants to do the will of God will know whether my teaching is from God or is merely my own."

God always gives His children a mouth and wisdom that the adversaries cannot contend and this wisdom is embedded in His commandments. When we delight ourselves in teaching and observing God's laws (instructions or commandments), we become wise and suddenly have the answers. The Jewish leaders in John 7:14 were asking about Jesus, *"How does he know so much when he hasn't studied everything we've studied?"* They did not know that Jesus did not need to study all they had studied because the all-knowing God lives in Him, and He is the wisdom of God. Jesus also knew the law of the Father.

There is something mystical about the laws of God that makes one know better than others.David understood this mystery by saying,

> *"I have better understanding and deeper insight than all my teachers because your testimonies are my meditation. I understand more than the aged (elders) because I keep Your precepts [hearing, receiving, loving, and obeying them]".*
> Psalm 119:99

Friends, no human or artificial intelligence can beat God's intelligence. Christ wanted us to experience this when He instructed us to teach and observe His commandments. God's kingdom is without borders of geographical location, race, ethnicity, religion, or civilisation. Every believer in the gospel of our Lord

Jesus is a citizen of that kingdom with an assignment to travel the world, which begins with our immediate environment, family, association, and workplace: teaching His commandments.

Jehoshaphat demonstrated kingdom influence by teaching and observing God's law throughout the towns of Judah, and God established him.

2 Chronicles 17:5-12

> *So, the LORD established Jehoshaphat's control over the kingdom of Judah. All the people of Judah brought gifts to Jehoshaphat, so he became very wealthy and highly esteemed. He was committed to the ways of the LORD. He knocked down the pagan shrines and destroyed the Asherah poles. In the third year of his reign, Jehoshaphat sent out his officials to teach in all the towns of Judah. These officials included Ben-hail, Obadiah, Zechariah, Nethanel, and Micaiah. He sent Levites along with them, including Shemaiah, Nethaniah, Zebadiah, Asahel, Shemiramoth, Jehonathan, Adonijah, Tobijah, and Tob-adonijah. He also sent out the priests, Elishama and Jehoram. They took copies of the Book of the Law of the LORD and travelled around all the towns of Judah, teaching the people. The fear of the LORD fell on all the kingdoms of the lands surrounding Judah so that they did not make war with Jehoshaphat.*

Some of the Philistines brought him gifts and silver as tribute, and the Arabs brought seventy-seven hundred rams and seventy-seven hundred male goats. So Jehoshaphat became increasingly powerful and built fortresses and store cities throughout Judah.

One way to destroy a kingdom or a nation is to encourage rebellion against that nation's laws (systems and structure). We must not forget that laws are made from the culture and values of a kingdom to protect her culture and values. The challenge is if these laws are not taught and enforced, there will be chaos and a complete breakdown of laws and order. This chaos and breakdowns have a subtle approach, and that approach is called influence.

If we must influence systems and institutions, we must reconsider teaching the Lord's laws (instructions, precepts, testimonies) as documented in the scriptures. Our value system must agree with God's, and His way must be our way. There are systems to be knocked down and voices to be silenced, no matter how strong and established they may be. When there is an invasion of truth, what seems established unshakeable shall be put off. Jehoshaphat built a strong resistance against idolatry and all kinds of vices in Jerusalem, not just by pulling down those shrines but by teaching the laws of the Lord in every corner of the towns in Jerusalem.

It is about time we take the word of God into our sectors. I don't mean organising fellowships and religious meetings in our workplace but seeing ourselves as the living word of life through our conduct and mannerisms and, most importantly, resisting unrighteous acts and everything ungodly. Resisting unrighteousness means enforcing righteousness, which is the kingdom of God. One of the ways to know we truly live is that people behold our glory (God's nature) through our demonstration of unfailing love, faithfulness, grace, and truth. This is kingdom influence.

Love

LOVE IS THE greatest. Our Lord Jesus summarised the laws and the prophets into two statements: love God with all your heart, soul, and mind, and love your neighbour as yourself, which means that the fulfilment of every commandment is love. God is love, and if we must bring God into every sector of human endeavour, it has to be through love. If the Kingdom of God must prosper in this perverted world, it can only be through the love of the Father. God's love drives our influence, manifesting in the new man we are in Christ.

2 Corinthians 5:14-15

> *Whatever we do, it is because Christ's love controls us. Since we believe that Christ died for everyone, we also believe that we have all died to the old life we used to live. He died for everyone so*

that those who receive his new life will no longer live to please themselves. Instead, they will live to please Christ, who died and was raised for them.

It is not because we do not enjoy the pleasure of sin; we now have a control switch in us as a result of the new life in Christ, which compels us to choose life over death. In other words, God's nature in us (love) judges us and also becomes the lens through which we have God's perception and position on every matter, and it is on this reality that we influence our world. Love is the greatest weapon of our influence, and He always wins. Love is God's way in every matter.

Romans 13:8-10

Owe no one anything except to love one another, for he who loves another has fulfilled the law. For the commandments, "You shall not commit adultery," "You shall not murder," "You shall not steal," "You shall not bear false witness," "You shall not covet," and if there is any other commandment, are all summed up in this saying, namely, "You shall love your neighbour as yourself."

Love does not harm a neighbour; therefore, love fulfils the law. We become catalysts for positive change when we submit and subject ourselves to God's love. All the anomalies in our society will stop if we engage ourselves, our duties, or our assignments with God's love. There will be no corrupt practices, immorality, or perversion where true love becomes the standard of living.

However, we know that if there is anything the world hates right now, it is the truth. Falsehood sells faster than truth, the offspring of God's love.

Don't forget that the only reason love compels us to do things is to establish God's way and position in that situation to the point that truth is enforced. So, God's love suffers so much attack to abort the truth. The reality is that doing things God's way attracts persecution, and what the enemy does not know is that these persecutions, trials, and tribulations provide us with a platform to express God's love (nature). This reality influences people around us, and if we are not relenting, our acts of God's love will raise a community of Christlike individuals who will continue to expand the frontiers of God's kingdom.

James 1:2-4

> *Consider it wholly joyful, my brethren, whenever you are enveloped in, encounter trials of any sort, or fall into various temptations. Be assured and understand that the trial and proving of your faith bring out endurance, steadfastness, and patience. But let endurance, steadfastness, and patience have full play and do thorough work so that you may be [people] perfectly and fully developed [with no defects], lacking in nothing.*

We rejoice in our hearts even amidst persecution, for we know that nothing can ever separate us from the love of God. We now share the same nature (love) with God, and our strength to withstand trials and temptation comes from His love in our hearts. While the world is trying to influence us with its lust and perversion, we influence the cosmos (the world and its inhabitants) with the love of God.

Apostle Paul, in one of his letters to the Galatians, highlighted the qualities (fruits) of God's love, and I believe these qualities are missing in our world today. Sometimes, we think these qualities are limited to church folks and forget that love is the fulfilment of the law. Whether the laws of institutions, nations, or communities, love is the fulfilment of laws. The way out of the breakdown of law and order is through love.

Galatians 5:22

> *The fruit of the spirit is love, joy, peace, patience, kindness, goodness, faithfulness, gentleness, and self- control. God is a spirit with the nature of love, and this nature has different expressions or qualities, such as joy, peace, patience, kindness, goodness, faithfulness, gentleness, and self-control.*

Love gives birth to the other fruits listed. These qualities are God's expression in and through us and are responsible for success and fulfilment in every human endeavour. I tell you, the only reason we can live happily with difficult bosses, husbands, and wives is that the joy of the Lord within strengthens us to overlook or pardon without any iota of resentment or bitterness.

There is a joy God's love produces in us even when there is nothing to be excited about in that relationship.

Peace also expresses God's love in our hearts, bringing calmness even in turbulent times. Peace is never an absence of storm. When two people fight over a matter, it simply means that one refuses to give peace a chance to reign. Peace is an expression of our confidence in God in any situation.

Patience is the strength of human relationships. It endures everything. Patience, or long-suffering, is a virtue that we can exude when dealing with difficult people. Kindness is fairness and equity of goodness, love, and every good virtue to all. It does not display favouritism. It is the tendency to consider others above oneself.

Goodness is compassion. The scriptures say of Jesus Christ, our Lord, that everywhere He went, He did good. Compassion triggers the anointing for the real virtue of service or impartation. To be faithful is to be full of faith. Faith has two components-believe and trust. Faithfulness is not reward-motivated. It is trust-motivated. Faithfulness is fidelity.

Gentleness is not a facial expression or look. It is the state of our minds and hearts, a stable mind. It is meekness and humility. Not having your way always, even when you have the power to do so, is humility.

A gentleman or woman does not enforce his or her will on people. Gentleness accommodates people's misconduct and flaws. The ability to let go and let God is gentleness. Just like patience, gentleness prevents anxiety and unnecessary curiosity. It brings stability to the mind. It is the gateway to receiving from God through faith.

Self-control is self-discipline. Setting boundaries allows one to stay focused and achieve a set goal. It is the ability to channel our energy, strength, or skills in the right direction. Wisdom is the bedrock of discipline. A fool never sees discipline as a virtue. Self-control is the strength of the spirit. Our influence becomes inevitable when we mirror these qualities of God's love in every sphere of human endeavour.

Chapter Seven

PURPOSE AND GREATNESS

Purpose is the essence of a thing. It is the primary duty or functionality of a thing. For instance, a microphone has the primary duty of amplifying voices. Irrespective of other substitute roles we might want a microphone to carry out, the truth is that the essence of a microphone is to amplify voices. In other words, the uniqueness of a microphone is the solution it offers that is peculiar to it. What is the significance of light without darkness? Light came into existence because of darkness.

With the illustration I have given, the manufacturer predetermines the purpose of a thing. That purpose is to find a solution that addresses a particular problem.

Jeremiah was born when God needed a prophet who would not compromise the truth for self-gain. There was a thick darkness of falsehood, and Jeremiah came as the light to remove that darkness.

Jeremiah 1:5 (AMP)

> *Before I formed you in the womb, I knew and approved of you [as My chosen instrument], and before you were born, I separated and set you apart, consecrated you, and appointed you as a prophet to the nations.*

Let us look at the word 'greatness'. Greatness has a few definitions, but I would like to limit the scope of this discussion to the meaning of greatness as distinction, eminence, renown, fame, and elevation. Greatness is the quality of being great.

It's what distinguishes an individual. It is tangible and can either be seen or felt. It's not peculiar to a group or class of people in society. Everyone can attain greatness.

Everyone who is great has something that distinguishes them. Beyond their vocation or profession, individuals discover what distinguishes them from their peers. Some refer to this discovery as a gift, talent, exceptional skill, education, or exposure; however, all of these are common factors that are not unique to an individual.

Gifts, talents, special skills, and education are a means to an end or outcome of one's life. There are tools that, when maximised, grant individuals access and the platform to manifest their essence.

Moreover, if we are characterised as gifted, educated, and exposed, it then means that our greatness is not a function of what we all have in common; instead, it is the solution they offer. Whatever makes you unique will definitely distinguish you. We live in a time where everyone wants to be popular, and most people struggle over this; some are even depressed because they are not famous like their friends. The dilemma is that we are confusing greatness with popularity or fame.

Greatness is a distinction that should not be misunderstood for competition or a contest. Your greatness is not competing with another man's greatness, so comparison is unnecessary.

We will never understand greatness if our perspective of greatness is an ideology of writing an exam and aiming for distinction or merit depending on our desires. Sometimes, it is assumed that whoever comes first in a contest is the greatest or that the man with the largest audience or followers is the greatest. The error in this mindset is that we start to think that greatness is all about our hard work, intellectual capability, smartness, or whatever an individual does.

Ecclesiastes 9:11 (NLT)

> *I have observed something else in this world of ours. The fastest runner doesn't always win the race, and the strongest warrior doesn't always win the battle. The wise are often poor, and the skillful are not necessarily wealthy. And those who are educated only sometimes lead successful lives. It is all decided by chance, by being at the right place and time.*

My focus on the above scripture is not the part that says, *"It is all decided by chance, but being at the right place and time."* I am trying to make us see that strength is good, education is necessary, and skill is highly needed, but none guarantees greatness. Greatness is guaranteed when we discover the compass that directs us to the right place and time. As humans, we must understand that, as highly intuitive or intelligent as we might be, our intuition is insufficient to direct our steps in the right direction. There is only one compass that leads and guides us to greatness: **Purpose**.

Purpose is the reason we exist and why we do the things we do. I have never seen a man who understood why he did the things he did and was never successful at what he did. Your whys become your motivation, even when it appears as if everything is falling apart. Your whys are what separate success from fulfilment. Accomplishing your whys gives you a feeling of fulfilment.

True greatness is born when we discover and consciously seek to fulfil

GOD'S PURPOSE FOR OUR LIVES

Greatness, Purpose, and Gift

I WANT US to see the relationship that binds our greatness, purpose, and gift together. Years ago, one of the youths in my local assembly visited me for a clarity session on the gift. His dilemma was knowing his dominant gift because he is a multitalented person. I started giving him God's counsel from his last statement: 'I am multitalented.' When we pay attention to ourselves as we grow, we will discover that talents seem to surface at every developmental stage, from infancy to adulthood. Most children, from toddlers to early teens, seem to love music and art while growing up because music is a natural therapy for children and aids learning.

So, music and art are talents that characterise childhood. At the teenage age, some lose interest in actively involving themselves in music and art. We see the talent of writing and speaking as having expression. It almost looks like the boy who said I wanted to be a pianist because of his love for music in his infant stage is now changing his mind to becoming a lawyer because he sees himself in that light due to the strength and power he newly discovered in his speaking and writing.

When the same child becomes an adult, he may discover some inherent abilities that may make him change his mind about what he thought he would become. Most of us are like this, and that is our definition of 'multitalent'. Undoubtedly, we have unlimited abilities that can make talents out of those abilities when we try to explore our inherent abilities. If we devote more time and resources to our talents, we can make gifts out of our talents.Talents are raw but, when polished and packaged, become presentable. Sometime, we see writers, singers, actors, and business people who are talented but have not mastered their craft and are not presenting their talents as gifts.

I want you to grab a cup of coffee, relax, and let's journey together. At this point, you will know if what you have is a talent or a gift. Is it possible to be multi-gifted? The answer is 'yes'. When we work on our inherent abilities and own them, they become gifts.Let me bring it to our attention that our talents are God's dimension of expressing Himself through us. God has a dimension of Himself that finds expression in nature, science, art, humanity, and technology. He put these expressions in us as talents, giving us the responsibility of cultivating them, mastering them, and presenting them as gifts. The gifts become keys that open specific doors, not all doors. I will explain this statement later.

It brings good feelings when we know that we are gifted, and that gift is a key that opens doors, right? It will be good to remind ourselves at this juncture that it is not about the gift but rather the giver of the gift. We worship the giver of the gift, not the gift. It is essential to understand the purpose. The purpose of the gift is also the purpose of the carrier of the gift. The purpose of the gift is to serve as a tool and also provide a platform for the carrier of the gift to do God's will. In other words, God's will becomes man's purpose, which is fulfilled through the instrumentality of His gift.

The gift is a tool for serving God and humanity in accordance with His will (leadership and guidance). How about those who think they are multigifted? My counsel to you is this: all the gifts in our lives have the primary purpose of helping us to fulfil God's will. For every one of His will that He wants us to carry out, there is a tool or an instrument (a gift) that helps.

Another thing you should look out for is to find the dominant gift among all your gifts and nurture it well. Most importantly, God's will is done through His gifts. Before I relate all of these to our greatness, I would like to reiterate that your gifts are tools and give you the platform to do God's will for your life. Let me also emphasise that the gifts, being a key, only open doors that align with God's purposes for your life. A man's gift makes room for him and brings him before great men.

Still, I also know of gifted persons who appeared before great men without a sense of purpose, thereby making an appearance that should last for a season only last for a short moment because the impression was never the will of God.

If God's purpose leads you to a place, every door in that space is automated with God's will as the access code. It is impossible to separate God's will from His purpose. God reveals His will and expects us to do it to work out His purposes for our lives. I always tell everyone around me who cares to believe that whether you were born with a silver spoon or not, there is greatness inside of you.

Regardless of the circumstances that preceded your birth, the good news is that you were born to be great. Everyone who dares to follow the will of God will experience greatness. Everyone has greatness, and the purpose of God for our lives creates a foundation and a platform for our greatness. The world or the community we belong to may have a way of putting people in different classes based on what they do, but I encourage us not to be bordered by how people view our greatness. Differences in greatness do not elevate one greatness above another but rather demonstrate one's uniqueness.

The Greatest Man Who Ever Lived

GOD'S PURPOSE FOR our lives is the compass for greatness. Our Lord Jesus chose to utilise heaven's investment in Him to fulfil His purpose. The Bible says our Lord Jesus has God's spirit without measure and the spirit of wisdom and understanding, counsel and might, knowledge and fear of the Lord. Imagine Christ investing all of these in carpentry- his father's business, in quest of being the wealthiest man that ever lived. He did not use His popularity, wisdom, and the grace of God upon His life to build an empire for Himself.

Jesus' life gave us a revelation of God's perspective on greatness. He knew that true greatness is total surrender to God's will. He knew He would never find greatness outside His essence. So, our Lord Jesus became the greatest man who ever lived not because of all the miracles He did but because of His death on the cross as the vicarious sacrifice for humanity's past, present, and future sins. This is God's perspective on greatness, accomplishing His purpose for our lives.

So, true greatness is accomplishing God's purposes for one's life. It is common sense to think that our lives will mirror those we learn from and the things we behold (feed our minds with). To become wealthy, observe the principles adopted by those with a track record of wealth, and if we desire true greatness, we can only learn from the one who is the greatest of all who has experienced life on this side of eternity: Jesus Christ our Lord. It is frustrating to have a burning desire to achieve something without knowing how to achieve it.The things we desperately pursued or desired at any cost were motivated by our quest for greatness, and there is this wrong notion about greatness as attaining the highest position, having our names in the world books such as Who is Who, Guinness Book of Record, Forbes and so on, that needs to be corrected. We should not settle for less and not be complacent with success, but I have a problem with how and the desperateness attached to becoming our desires.

Many are innocently frustrated today because they got it all twisted, thinking that man's desires make him great, and they have suffered countless losses because of their ignorance. It is the will of God that makes us great. Position, wealth, and influence gotten outside God's will can never make us great. Let's not be deceived; there is a lot we cannot achieve on our own. We can't be famous and celebrated without God. The scripture calls it ways that seem right (not God's will) in our own eyes but ultimately bring destruction.

I want us to observe a fundamental principle our Lord Jesus taught His disciples about greatness. Just as we are, the disciples were also concerned about positions and who becomes the greatest among them.

Mark 10:35-45

Then James and John, the sons of Zebedee, came over and spoke to him. "Teacher," they said, "we want you to do us a favour." "What is it?"

He asked. "In your glorious Kingdom, we want to sit in places of honour next to you," they said, "one at your right and the other at your left." But Jesus answered, "You don't know what you are asking! Are you able to drink from the bitter cup of sorrow I am about to drink? Are you able to be baptised with the baptism of suffering I must be baptised with?" "Oh yes," they said, "we are able!" And Jesus said, "You will indeed drink from my cup and be baptised with my baptism, but I have no right to say who will sit on the thrones next to mine. God has prepared those places for the ones he has chosen." They were indignant when the ten other disciples discovered what James and John had asked. So, Jesus called them together and said, "You know that in this world, kings are tyrants, and officials lord it over the people beneath them. But among you, it should be quite different. Whoever wants to be a leader among you must be your servant, and whoever wants to be first must be the slave of all. For even I, the Son of Man, came here not to be served but to serve others and to give my life as a ransom for many."

The first lesson from Jesus' submission to their quest for position and greatness is that God only does His will for us and through us. He does not favour the desires of our flesh. God does nothing for man except His will. The second lesson is that the only way to know what to do or what to ask for is to ask the Father to reveal His will to us on every matter. Jesus made the disciples know that what was ordained for them is more significant than the price, and the fact that the price is inevitable does not mean greatness could be achieved outside what the Father has ordained.

There is so much emphasis on capacity building and cost for whatever we desire to achieve, and this may not always be the right approach to greatness. There is the bitter cup of sorrow and the baptism of suffering that come with fulfilling God's purpose for our lives, but how do you explain the sorrow of one who is going in the opposite direction of God's will and, in the process, lost everything? Godly sorrow is inevitable as we journey with God to achieve His purposes for our lives.

Apostle Paul gave us an insight into fighting with purpose in view. He said,

> *"All athletes practice strict self-control. They do it to win a prize that will fade away, but we do it for an eternal prize. So, I run straight to the goal with purpose in every step. I am not like a boxer who misses his punches. I discipline my body like an athlete, training it to do what it should. Otherwise, I fear that after preaching to others, I myself might be disqualified." (1 Corinthians 9:25–27)*

Apostle Paul says that if there is anything that should be our target, focus, and motivation, let it be what the Father has chosen for us. Apostle Paul is saying to us in this text that it is obvious that desires are calling our attention to want them, but he has chosen to fight for the Father's desire (God's purpose) for his life. He admonished us to practice strict self-control while building capacity or putting up for a fight. We should not forget that the things that count for greatness align with God's purposes for our lives. Self-control allows God's will to interject our carnal ambitions on every matter. Do we need to build capacity? Yes, but let it be in the things that will launch us deeper into God's will for our lives. Nothing is as good as labouring for what the Father has chosen (ordained) for us.

The third lesson in Jesus' conversation with the disciples regarding position and greatness is that greatness comes with self-denial: denying oneself of comfort and pleasure to serve or make others better. Jesus said, "For even I, the Son of man, came here not to be served but to serve others and give my life as a ransom for many." This statement by our Lord Jesus should be our mindset if we truly desire greatness. Christ's ultimate purpose was captured in the statement: to give His life as a ransom for us. Apostle Paul's letters to the Philippians explained how our Saviour attained greatness.

Philippians 2:5-11 (AMPC)

> *Let this same attitude and purpose and [humble] mind be in you which was in Christ Jesus: [Let Him be your example in humility:] Who, although being essentially one with God and in the form of God [possessing the fullness of the attributes which make God God], did not think this equality with God was a thing to be eagerly grasped or retained, but stripped Himself [of all privileges and rightful dignity], so as to assume the guise of a servant (slave), in that He became like men and was born a human being. And after He had appeared in human form, He abased and humbled Himself [still further] and carried His obedience to the extreme of death, even the death of the cross! Therefore [because He stooped so low] God has highly exalted Him and has freely bestowed on Him the name that is above every name, that in (at) the name of Jesus every knee should (must) bow, in heaven and on earth and under the earth, And every tongue [frankly and openly] confess and acknowledge that Jesus Christ is Lord, to the glory of God the Father.*

From this text, we can see that it was not the miracles our Saviour performed that got Him the greatest name; instead, it was His obedience to God's purpose for His life. He became so great that demons and all spirits acknowledge His Lordship and bow to the authority of His name. The scriptures give a powerful remark about

David that I would like us to remember whenever the desire to be great comes to mind.

Psalm 78:72

So [David] was their shepherd with an upright heart; he guided them by the discernment and skillfulness [which controlled] his hands.

Acts 13:36

For David, after he had served God's will and purpose and counsel in his own generation, fell asleep [in death] and was buried among his forefathers, and he did see corruption and undergo putrefaction and dissolution [of the grave].

David met the condition for greatness. He served his generation with heart integrity (uprightness). And he did so by serving them according to God's will and purpose for his life. He led them by discerning God's will; this is contrary to our perception of greatness. We know of kings who use their power to oppress people and force them to do their will rather than God's will. They fail to recognise that true greatness is measured not by wealth and power but by humility in serving others regardless of position or possession.

What we accomplish for God and His kingdom in accordance with His will makes us great, not what we accomplish for ourselves. Some would say their good works to humanity conferred greatness on them. It is a great deception to associate greatness with wealth, charitable works, and any type of influence (political, social, or economic) an individual has over a territory. If our goodwill is not motivated by God's will and does not benefit God's kingdom, it will never be considered great in God's eyes. God is more concerned with why we do what we do (motive), and if our motives are God-directed, they will benefit His kingdom.

I admonish you, friends, to choose God's will above works. Often, God's will may not make us popular or famous, but it does bring fulfilment and eternal rest with the Father.

Matthew 7:21-23 (NLT)

> *"Not all people who sound religious are really godly. They may refer to me as 'Lord,' but they still won't enter the Kingdom of Heaven. The decisive issue is whether they obey my Father in heaven. On judgment day, many will tell me, 'Lord, Lord, we prophesied in your name and cast out demons in your name and performed many miracles in your name.' But I will reply, 'I never knew you. Go away; the things you did were unauthorised."*

I realised from these scriptures that what we do in the name of Jesus is not the Father's goal. It is the things that we do under His authority that count. We may build churches, finance the gospel, engage in charitable works, heal the sick, raise the dead, and so on. The question we must ask ourselves is, under whose authority are we doing the things we do? Will Jesus say to you, "Go away; the things you did were unauthorised."

Chapter Eight

A DEATH SENTENCE

A carnal man cannot respond to the call or the assignment of God for his life. God's purpose is glamorous, but it is deadly. I call it the right death for man. Our fame, prosperity, and every fulfilling moment of life are tied to our assignment, but all of these do not make it less deadly. Everyone taking this assignment must be ready to die to self and worldliness. Our Lord Jesus is a perfect example of this. For Christ, the way to glory was through His sufferings and pains. He was stigmatised, brutalised, and hung on the cross. The horror of His death has produced many saints and sons of God today, including you and me, if you have accepted Him as your Lord and Saviour.

Acts 9: 16

> *"For I will shew him how great things he must suffer for my name's sake."*

This is the testimony that accompanied Paul's ministry. A cup is prepared for everyone who must accept God's assignment for their lives. We all need to drink from this cup. Many believe that Apostle Paul went through all of the hardship because he persecuted the church before discovering the truth, but this is not correct. Our Lord Jesus suffered so much, and the question is: What sin did He commit? Many today attribute the pain they go through to the life they lived before they gave their lives to Christ. The truth is that our sins have been forgiven; God lost the memory of our past when we accepted Christ. Yes, there may be some scars from our past, but the truth is that our realities in Christ have no connection with our past. If God and greatness are now our brands, we must be willing to drink from the same cup our Master drank from that birthed glory and greatness.

Philippians 1:29

> *"For to you, it has been granted on behalf of Christ, not only to believe in Him but also to suffer for His sake,"*

Our Lord Jesus told James and John in Mark 10:39, *"You will indeed drink the cup that I drink, and with the baptism that I am baptised with, you will be baptised."* He said this when they asked Him to grant them the privilege to sit at the right and left hand of Christ in His Glory.

Therefore, when we see ourselves suffering for the right course, maybe persecuted for preaching the gospel, denial of our benefits for not engaging in corrupt practices, and all sorts of challenges from family and workplace because of our allegiance to Christ, we must see these as righteous suffering. They have nothing to do with our past; they are all part of the process that will birth greatness and glory. It's all part of our new creation realities.

It is Worth the Fight: Fight For it

SOMEONE ASKED ME, "Why would God send Lucifer out of heaven to the earth He has given to man to subdue and dominate?" My simple answer to that question is – God did that to subject Lucifer to the highest degree of humiliation because He knew the devil would soon find his place under the feet of man through the redemption of man. In chapter one, I spoke about the ideal man that existed in God's mind before the earth's creation.

Ephesians 1:3-4

> *Blessed be the God and Father of our Lord Jesus Christ, who has blessed us with every spiritual blessing in the heavenly places in Christ, just as He chose us in Him before the foundation of the world.*

Before the earth's foundation, a lamb was also slain (Jesus Christ, the second person in the Trinity). "*All who dwell on the earth will worship Him, whose names have not been written in the Book of Life of the Lamb slain from the foundation of the world.*" (Revelation 13:8)

God, in His Omniscience, did all of these, knowing that the devil would seek out the ideal man after his creation and cause him to rebel against God's commands. So, after the creation of man, the deceiver (Satan) corrupted him, and the Almighty God decreed Satan's humiliation and irreversible destruction. Man, however, can atone for his rebellion.

Genesis 3:10-15

> *So he said, "I heard Your voice in the garden, and I was afraid because I was naked, and I hid myself." And He said, "Who told you that you were naked? Have you eaten from the tree of which I commanded you that you should not eat?" Then the man said, "The woman whom You gave to be with me, she gave me of the tree, and I ate." And the LORD God said to the woman, "What is this*

you have done?" The woman said, "The serpent deceived me, and I ate." So the LORD God said to the serpent: "Because you have done this, You are cursed more than all cattle, And more than every beast of the field; On your belly, you shall go, And you shall eat dust All the days of your life. And I will put enmity Between you and the woman, And between your seed and her seed; He shall bruise your head, And you shall bruise his heel."

Why would Satan cause separation between God and man? Is it to make the earth inhabitable for man or prove that as long as man lives on earth, he is subject to his control? I believe Satan intended to hinder God's will on earth. Therefore, he came after the image of God (man), who has the mandate to enforce the will of God. Jesus calls Satan a destroyer, and the only thing he targets to destroy is the essence of man (God's image). Friends, Satan is against anyone who thrives to do the will of God, and he is on the rampage, never tired to ensure that he fulfils his essence.

John 10:10

"The thief does not come except to steal, and to kill, and to destroy. I have come that they may have life and that they may have it more abundantly".

Jesus is telling us that the only reason Satan comes is to steal, kill, and destroy. I have never seen any serious-minded thief who comes to steal things that are not valuable. The thief comes prepared to steal what gives us life and the things that keep us going. Let me announce to you, friends: Satan has come to steal what Jesus had given us. Remember, I told us that Jesus led us to the Father so we can access His will for our lives, which means that the satisfying and abundant life Jesus gives comes from the will of the Father. Have you wondered why the ungodly seems to be prospering? They seem to have everything they want, and they even oppress the Godly with their successes and so on.

The ungodly is that man who has submitted himself to Satan as his co-labourer to go against the will of God. The godly should always remind himself that the prosperity of the ungodly does not bring satisfaction. It may satisfy their body, but it does bring destruction to the mind and soul. There is a battle over man's soul, which is the fight he must fight. The ungodly is not in any battle with Satan, but that does not make him Satan's friend. Satan has an incurable hatred for man, and he is determined to kill man. All he needs to do is to contaminate man with sin and make him defenceless to the repercussions of sin (death).I want us to ponder on this statement: 'Satan has an incurable hatred for man, and if he did not spare those who are loyal to his will and have who also have become his co-labourers aiding to increase the frontiers of his kingdom, how then will he spare God's children?' we can see that the battle line has been drawn.

Genesis 3:15

> *And I will put enmity between you and the woman, and between your seed and her seed; he shall bruise your head, and you shall bruise his heel."*

Here is the good news for the child of God. The Bible calls this fight a good fight of faith. A fight can only be good if you win it, but it would be a bad one for the man who lost it. So, this fight is good because it ends in our victory as children of God.Moreover, it is also a good fight of faith. Faith is compelling. Faith is a substance, and it is evidence of the ideal man in the mind of God before the earth's foundation. This ideal man is the will of God for His image (man), and it is what we fight for. In case you are wondering, what is this ideal man in the mind of God? The ideal man is the man who is perfect in beauty, blameless, holy, and shares the same nature with God (a little lower than God); he understands the purpose of every creature. He is crowned with glory and is the man with the mandate of dominion and the authority conferred on him.

Imagine if we all become the ideal men God intended before creation; the earth will become heaven. Is it not a good fight? I am pleading with you, my brothers, and my sisters to fight for it, for it is worth the fight.

1 Timothy 6:12

> *"Fight the good fight of faith, lay hold on eternal life, to which you were also called, and have confessed the good confession in the presence of many witnesses".*

Another good news about this fight is that our victory was decided long ago. Jesus Christ, the Lamb of God, was slain before the foundation of the earth as the vicarious sacrifice that gave us victory. Our faith is in the vicarious sacrifice of the Lamb, who is our victory. He bruised the head of the serpent (the deceiver) and put him under our feet.

Purpose and Pleasure

GOD IS NOT against us having leisure time. We can spend our leisure time relaxing, watching a movie, reading a book, or meditating. As children of God, we must remember that God wants to be involved in using our time. He would like to be there when we are having fun. We must ensure that what we do with our time gives Him glory. God will never be present wherever He is not given the due glory to His name. Adam and Eve did not invite God in those times, and He came to visit them in the Garden of Eden. God always came around because the things they did gave Him glory.

The responsibility of tilling the garden is God's ultimate goal for them. God is pleased, so He comes to visit. God stopped visiting them the day the serpent enticed them to do something they weren't supposed to do, and the last time He came was for judgement. Adam and Eve were condemned to death. The use of our time either glorifies or insults God. God is omnipresent, meaning He sees all that man does but does not partake of everything. He only manifests Himself where He will receive the glory, and for Him to receive the glory that is due to His name, the things we do must be pleasurable in His sight. My pleasure must not hinder God's pleasure. It should not offend or insult God. When I hang out with unbeliever friends in public and private places, drinking and feasting even when I am not drinking alcohol, smoking a cigarette, or flirting with women, the truth is that I am already sitting in the seat of the scornful.

Psalms 1:1 (AMP)

> *Blessed (happy, fortunate, prosperous and enviable) is the man who walks and lives not in the counsel of the ungodly(following their advice, their plans, and purposes)nor stands (submissive and inactive) in the path where sinners walk, nor sit down (relax and rest) where the scornful (and the mockers) gather.*

What glory is God receiving from me by that act? What I read, watch, and listen to, how are they giving God glory? Going to nightclubs with friends, going to cinemas to see ungodly movies with friends, my conversation, or gist, and so on, how did God receive glory in all of these?

1 Corinthians 6:19

"Know ye not that your body is the temple of the Holy Spirit."

My body is the compartment that houses my spirit (God's Spirit within me) and my soul. What I do with my body matters to God. I know you are a virgin; you have never had any physical intercourse with the opposite sex, but you have had several intercourses spiritually through the things you watched, read, and heard. Just as sexual sin defiles the body, spirit, and soul, so also are the things we do with our time when we are not giving God the glory due to His name defiling our body, soul, and spirit.

"Having the form of godliness, denying the power thereof" is the case of many believers. We must know that religion promotes hypocrisy and carnality. Christianity (exhibiting a Christ-like nature) encourages the demonstration of His power.

Chapter Nine

THE LAW OF FOCUS

The word focus is only practicable in a life with purpose in view. Purpose produces vision. I used to tell my students that any vision outside God's purpose for their lives makes them victims. We can't sweep this statement under the carpet because vision is critical to the destination. So, before casting a vision, we should seek God's will. The purpose is the end goal, and it is for this reason that we can create a vision to guide us there, a mission to lead us there, and goals to bring that end into the present. It is crucial that we recognise that our purpose defines us, influences our decisions, reveals our uniqueness, and forms the basis of our brand. Purpose is our voice and the message we convey.

If God's purpose is all I have highlighted, it implies that finding and fulfilling God's purpose for our lives is a serious business.

If you are reading this and have found purpose, I encourage you to focus on your purpose; if you have not found it, I admonish you to talk to the Father about it. Without a specific purpose, everything captures an individual's attention. The tragedy about not walking in God's purpose is that it makes us victims of pathways that seem right, but the end is destruction.

God's purpose is like a plough we should hold onto and never look back. Purpose has a jealous nature. It does not want us to share our time and affection with something else. It is very demanding but rewarding and requires us to focus all our attention on fulfilling God's purpose. I would like to use focus as an acronym for principles that keep us on the journey of purpose.

Applying the law of focus helps us navigate through life with ease. We only have one life to live. Life is one opportunity that, once lost, can never be restored. So, it is essential to know that we cannot experiment with the only life we have to live. I would like to highlight the **3S** of life we all experience, which also signifies different phases of our journey through life. These three **'S'** also show our perspectives on life.

The first **'S'** is **struggle** or **shuffle:** For most of us, life is a struggle, a fight that seems not to end. There is so much confusion with life's choices; everything looks like a misfit. Unfortunately, this is the first phase of life for everyone, regardless of your background, whether you were born with a silver spoon or not. I call it the first compactment or phase of life. Tough decisions are made in this phase, which can either bail us out of this phase or keep us in this phase. So, this phase has no expiration time. The whole of one's life can be spent moving in cycles without coming out of this phase. A rat race, unhealthy comparison, no sense or feeling of fulfilment, and a mood swing between depression and short-term happiness characterise the struggle phase.

Anyone who desires to see beyond this phase must find answers to the following questions: Who am I? Who is my source? Why am I here? And what is my contribution to my generation? The answers to these questions give us the resilient spirit that moves us into the next phase.

The next phase is the **success phase:** One thing about this phase is that not everyone sees or experiences it. This is the stage where we become pragmatic and intentional with who we are, why we are here, and what we carry (potentials and talents). The road is not smooth at this point, but the things we've learned about ourselves keep us going, regardless of the roughness of the road or the difficulties that come with it. We approach this phase with clear ideas of who we are and the one thing that defines our essence. In the struggle phase, people are fond of trying everything to be successful, and they are not; instead, they become frustrated. In the success phase, we do everything to be successful.

Here is the difference: to try everything means trying things we are not sure of the outcome, but to do everything means that there is this identity of mine that I know the outcome. I'm doing everything possible to make that outcome my reality. The success phase is characterised by sacrifice, but the sacrifice means nothing to us because there is an outcome—a glorious end in view. On this understanding, our difficulties, pains, and trials become a motivation, not a discouragement. We look beyond the pains and discomforts our sacrifice will cost us because we have seen the glory we should become. Friends, if you are in this phase right now, your success is guaranteed, and I encourage you to meditate daily on the word of God.

Hebrews 12: 2 (MSB)

Keep your eyes on Jesus, who both began and finished this race we're in. Study how He did it. Because He never lost sight of where He was headed, that exhilarating finish in and with God, He could put up with anything along the way:

cross, shame, whatever. And now He's there, in the place of honour, right alongside God.

The last phase is the **significance phase:** At this phase, our approach to life is about what we accomplish for God, our source and the giver of all we have acquired. This phase is significant because it is purpose-driven and crucial to ensuring that all our accomplishments align with God's ordination and plans. It is no longer about our comfort, personal success, or gains. It is a phase where we keep searching to see that nothing is left unused. The truth is that both the success and significance phases are meant to break out simultaneously. We are not waiting to be very successful in our endeavours before we start to think of making a significant influence that will outlive us and transcend generations to come. Success gives personal fulfilment, while significance gives God the fulfilment of the essence of our existence.

As I said earlier, struggle, success, and significance are all life's perspectives, giving different feelings to life. What you call a struggle can become someone's motivation to discover what will become a good fight because he finally laid hold on the eternal things. I admonish you to find your good fight and trust God for grace to win the prize.

2 Timothy 4:7-8 (AMP)

I have fought the good [worthy, honourable, and noble] fight; I have finished the race, I have kept [firmly held] the faith.[As to what remains] henceforth, there is laid up for me the [victor's] crown of righteousness [for being right with God and doing right], which the Lord, the righteous Judge, will award to me and recompense me on that [great] day - and not to me only, but also to all those who have loved and yearned for and welcomed His appearing [His return].

Apostle Paul's testimony of finishing strong would not have surfaced in the pages of the scriptures if he had lost focus along the way. The word focus for me is not just a word. I believe it is more of a collection of principles. Focus survives the test of time, from struggle to significance. I will use the word focus as an acronym for a collection of principles that keep us through the journey.

F- Faith

O- Optimistic

C- Concentration and Commitment

U- Usefulness

S- Sacrifice

Focus guarantees significance. Just like driving a car, when you lose focus and allow distraction to set in, it will lead to a fatal accident that will cost you your life, but when you concentrate on the journey, you will reach your desired destination. Let us begin with the first word in the acronym.

Faith

FAITH IS CRITICAL for change. When hopelessness meets faith in our hearts, new realities are made. The voidness of the earth did not prevent the Creator from having the experience He had envisioned before time; He brought those experiences or realities into being. That is the power of faith. If you trust God and believe what He has predestined for your life, I tell you that is what will be. Faith in God and His promises for our lives will keep us on course, regardless of the obstacles before us.

Isaiah 50:7

> *Because the sovereign Lord helps me, I will not be dismayed. Therefore, I have set my face like a stone, determined to do His will. And I know that I will triumph.*

A purpose-driven life is an adventure that can take us through a few detours as we embark on this journey. We just set God and His will before us and be resolute to do nothing but His counsel. Distractions are inevitable, but with the power of focus through faith in God and His word, we will stay on course.When everything looks like you will not make it, do not shift your ground; boast in your God, watch out for His instructions, and stand on His promises. So, when I am going through hard times in the process of becoming what God said about me, all I need to do is look at Jesus and not myself. Someone said, "But I must believe in myself". Yes, believe in yourself.

What that means is that you believe in the abilities of God in you. You are an endowment of abilities. You are up to the task, so don't be afraid. God's abilities in us are up to the task, so believe.

Optimistic

TO BE OPTIMISTIC is to wave off every negative energy that can quickly slow us down, setting our eyes on God's purpose and plans. The picture of the future in our minds is what becomes our reality. It is essential to set our eyes on purpose. Do not be afraid of the journey. Keep your assurance that no matter how rough the journey to greatness is, everything works for the best. The Bible in Romans 8:28 says all things are working together for your good. Affirm God's word to yourself, knowing that denial is not God's nature and that He is ever faithful to His promises. The scriptures describe Abraham's confidence in God's promise of becoming the father of many nations. Abraham's reality contradicted God's promise. Nonetheless, he stood firm on God's promise: "I will make you a father of many nations."

Commitment and Contentment

COMMITMENT IS BINDING oneself (intellectually or emotionally) to a course of action. To be committed is to give undivided attention to a task. As the saying goes, there are two individuals in the world, and these individuals are either making things happen or watching things happen, and those who make things happen do it with an absolute commitment to the task before them. Let's take, for instance, an athlete whose mandate is to win a medal and who will not entertain excuses or anything that will truncate that mandate. So, he will devote much time to ensuring his mandate is actualised. When we devote certain hours of the day to cultivating God's purpose for our lives, upscaling or sharpening our gifts and skills to help us fulfil His specific mandates, it helps us stay on course. I have not seen anyone committed to doing God's will and lacking anything good. Just as the reward for work is more work, likewise, the reward for obedience is more obedience, but not without God's grace. *"For the Lord God is a sun and shield; the Lord will give grace and glory; no good thing will He withhold from those who walk uprightly."* Psalm 84:1

Galatians 6:9

> *"And let us not lose heart and grow weary and faint in acting nobly and doing right, for in due time and at the appointed season; we shall reap if we do not loosen and relax our courage and faint."*

As long as we keep doing the right thing, we will win. There is another dimension to our commitment to doing the will of God; it is called contentment. Our focus on God's mandate can be compromised if we lack contentment. We must learn to be content with every milestone we achieve in the pursuit of our assignment. The whole idea is to set our eyes on the finish line. The journey of purpose is a marathon race. We must endure to the end. Contentment does not mean we should not desire more or higher milestones. As long as it aligns with the blueprint and the motive is not to satisfy our ego. Whatever a man is committed to is an assurance of being fruitful.

Contentment helps us set boundaries. God's purpose is very glamorous and puts every man who finds it on the front line of relevance and influence with loud homage and ovation. At this point, contentment is very critical. It must be the guard we must employ to avoid crossing the lines. I have seen people called into the ministry of raising men, planting churches, disciplining people, and building men who will become potters of ideas that will change their world. They were very committed to this assignment until contentment lost its hold on them one day. They begin to see their popularity and fame. The wrong motive in their hearts created a detour on the assignment that was given at first and ended up running a completely different vision that wasn't the blueprint.

Chapter Nine

Usefulness

THE JOURNEY FROM struggle to significance has one mission to accomplish: satisfaction. Satisfaction is a feeling of fulfilment. The question is, why do we crave satisfaction, and it seems it's out of reach? The simple answer is that we are chasing either needs or wants. Needs are of God, while wants are of men. God's intention for creating man was to meet His needs. He packaged those needs in us as talents to serve His purposes. So, individuals are packaged with specific needs to serve God's purposes.

Unfortunately, man's failure to recognise God's needs as his own alters his perception of doing everything to meet his needs, and not knowing what he needs leads to insatiable cravings for his desires (wants). What is the way forward? The way forward is to ask ourselves about God's will and plans. God's will determines our usefulness; it leads us to where we are needed and how we can be useful to meet God's needs. We will overcome a large percentage, if not all, of the things that got us distracted when we understand this truth. I have realised that our biggest distraction are those activities we involve ourselves in that abuse our usefulness. It is like putting a round peg in a square hole.

We become more productive to ourselves and God when we limit our activities to only those things that require our input and express the problems or needs that we were created to solve or meet. Most of the activities we engage in are either self-driven or want-driven, leaving us with holes in our hearts that can never be filled unless we embrace God's needs. Human needs are insatiable because there is no way to measure them, so they become wants that do not provide satisfaction. Only God's needs (our essence) can provide satisfaction.

Sacrifice

SACRIFICE IS A choice we must make. Some cannot come out of their struggle because they are not ready to sacrifice their comfort for the success they desire. Man's nature is always looking for the easy way out or shortcuts to success, which is largely responsible for bad outcomes. To a large extent, we all agree that we must sit down and count the cost before embarking on a project, but occasionally, we seek the easy way out after we have counted our cost. Therefore, our choices are largely responsible for the outcome or what we make out of life. The scripture in Deuteronomy 30:15 says, "I place before you today life and death. I admonish you to choose life".

To pick life is to select the path that leads to life, and to decide life is to decide to submit to the plan of God for our lives; going God's way means we must abandon our ways, let go of our comfort, pleasure, self and embrace God's processes that will bring out His best deposited in us. There are many things we think we want but are only wishes. Wishes are fantasies or dreams that have no desire to be realised, whereas desires are realities that we are determined to bring to life, and that determination is known as passion, and it will cost us something. Everyone is afraid to sacrifice, even though they understand the cost and consequences of not sacrificing, but they are torn between the two options.

People experiencing poverty are afraid of sacrificing their little comfort and complacency in exchange for the success they desire. The rich are afraid of sacrificing their possessions and successes in exchange for significance (true fulfilment). They keep acquiring more, and they never think of deploying what they have acquired. To be fulfilled in life requires some form of sacrifice, and anyone who fails to sacrifice is like a man who found a treasure and refused to sell off all that he has to have the treasure. The man probably refused to sacrifice his comfort, pleasure, ungodly relationship, and time in exchange for the treasure.

Mark 10:28-31 (AMPC)

> *Peter started to say to Him, Behold, we have yielded up [sacrifice] and abandoned everything [once and for all and joined You as Your disciples, siding with Your party] and accompanied You [walking the same road that You walk]. Jesus said, Truly I tell you, there is no one who has given up and left house or brothers or sisters or mother or father or children or lands for My sake and for the Gospel's Who will not receive a*

hundred times as much now in this time–houses and brothers and sisters and mothers and children and lands, with persecutions–and in the age to come, eternal life.

If we do God's will, we must follow in the footsteps of the Master, and this comes at a cost. As Christ, our Saviour, says, there is an assurance of a hundredfold return of what we sold off in exchange for the fulfilment of His will and purposes for our lives. Therefore, I say to you, friends, stay **FOCUS**. I mean, be full of **FAITH** - in His will and plans for your life, be **OPTIMISTIC** - wave off every doubt, discouragement, and all kind of negative vibes around you, be **COMMITTED** to His ways and purposes for your life, consecrate yourself to God, be **CONTENT** with His will, understand your **USEFULNESS** as described by His will and finally, be ready to **SACRIFICE**.

Christ paid the ultimate sacrifice; He took our sins, shame, diseases, and affliction, died the death we should have died, and gave us His life (free of sin and corruption) so that we may live for Him. What is the life of Christ? The summary of the life of our Lord Jesus is in His words.

John 5:19 (NKJV)

Then Jesus answered and said to them, "Most assuredly, I say to you, the Son can do nothing of Himself, but what He sees the Father do;

for whatever He does, the Son also does in like manner.

Even at the most difficult moment of His life, Christ chose to do the will of His Father (God).

Luke 22:42 (NLT)

"Father, if you are willing, please take this cup of suffering away from me. Yet I want your will to be done, not mine."

Jesus is telling us that the real essence of our lives is to do the will of God.

FINAL NOTES

The journey of exploring purpose has brought us to profound realisations and revelations that redemption is the prerequisite for seeking God. Purpose is not a destination to be reached; it is a constant evolution. It is a driving force that ignites our souls, compelling us to take meaningful action and live a life aligned with the will of God. It is through connecting with our purpose that we tap into a wellspring of strength and resilience, propelling us forward even in the face of adversity. This book is a reminder that fuels and drives us out of mediocrity and towards a life of significance and meaning. As we close this chapter, let us carry with us the wisdom and inspiration found within these pages. Let us continue to seek, cultivate, and share our purpose with unwavering passion and dedication. In doing so, we unlock the limitless potential that resides within us and forge a path illuminated by purpose, love, and fulfilment.

In the end, we all have a purpose in life, even if we don't always know what it is. The journey to discovering our purpose can be challenging, but it's worth it to find the thing that truly fulfils us. No matter where you are on your path, keep seeking out the will of God, and you'll find your essence in life. It might not be what you expected, but it will be worth it in the end, for God knows your end from your beginning. You don't have to follow a script or formula to find your purpose - follow the word of God and do what is right.

UNLOCKING PURPOSE

"Unlocking Purpose" is a remarkable book that underscores the significance of embracing God's intentions for our existence. The book provides valuable guidance on discovering your purpose in life and manifesting your true potential. It also incorporates the powerful law of FOCUS - Faith, Optimism, Contentment, Usefulness, and Service - to help readers achieve their goals with unwavering determination. The beauty of "Unlocking Purpose" lies in its profound message and practical approach to life discovery. The book is a comprehensive manual that can help you become the ideal person God created. Its pages are filled with inspiring words of wisdom that can catalyze positive change in your personal and professional life. Through "Unlocking Purpose," readers can gain insights into how they can align their lives with God's plans and fulfill their destiny. The book emphasizes the importance of living a purpose-driven life, one that is centered around faith, hope, and love. It encourages readers to embrace their uniqueness as the power to transform lives and inspire greatness.

ABOUT THE AUTHOR

Oluwasanmi Dada is a member of Kingdom Life Seminar, an interdenominational fellowship aimed at following the footprints of Jesus. He is also a community chaplain and a Perazim School of Chaplaincy alumnus. He is happily married to Tolulope Dada, and they are blessed with two children, David and Olivette.

Published by:
PEN-IMPACT WRITING
& PUBLISHING ENTERPRISE

ISBN 978-978-788-230-6
9 789787 882306

www.ingramcontent.com/pod-product-compliance
Lightning Source LLC
LaVergne TN
LVHW091329150826
845673LV00006B/1814

* 9 7 8 9 7 8 7 8 8 2 3 0 6 *